PENGUIN BOOKS

THE ECONOMICS OF SMALL THINGS

Sudipta Sarangi is a professor of economics at Virginia Tech. His research interests include networks, development economics and behavioural economics. He has been a consultant to the World Bank and the Food and Agriculture Organization of the United Nations, and serves on the editorial board of several journals. He enjoys teasing out economic insights from the little things in life. Currently, he hosts *Coffee with the Chair*, a virtual programme for undergraduate students at his university who are interested in all things economics. He grew up in Rourkela, which he remembers fondly and still loves to visit. He has lived in two of the most important cities in the world—Delhi, as a student before moving to the United States for his doctoral studies, and Washington DC, where he was a programme director at the National Science Foundation. He currently lives in Blacksburg, a small town nestled in the mountains of Southwest Virginia, with his wife, daughter and their dog Duffly. Among his favourite cities are Berlin in the summer, Paris all year round and Istanbul for its views and culinary delights. He also enjoys music, reading, writing and playing silly games with his daughter that they invent together.

ADVANCE PRAISE FOR THE BOOK

'In this charming, magical book, Sarangi shows that economics matter in our daily life. In little things, in little lives—in offering prayers, buying mangoes, watching movies, guarding shoes at the temple, wearing seatbelts. This book is economics as great entertainment!'

—Gurcharan Das, bestselling author and former CEO of Procter & Gamble India

'Economists generally think of their audience as other economists. But in this book Sudipta Sarangi takes on the far more important task of explaining to a broader audience how the world—in all its everyday, quirky, rich detail—can be understood through the prism of economics.

It is daring, illuminating and entertaining at the same time. And you can even find out whether Mahatma Gandhi's complaint against the Indian Railways was economically well-founded.'

—Arvind Subramanian, former chief economic advisor
to the Government of India and a non-resident fellow of
the Peterson Institute of International Economics

'In *The Economics of Small Things*, Sudipta Sarangi shows how a few simple principles of human behaviour can help us in understanding an extraordinarily diverse range of interesting phenomena in our day-to-day lives. He writes with humour and a lightness of touch that is remarkable. The book is perfectly pitched—enlightening and delightfully readable!'

—Sanjeev Goyal, professor of economics, University of Cambridge

'Always wanted to know why the best Indian Alphonso mangoes seem affordable in American grocery stores but expensive in India? Or why India never had the proliferation of Blockbuster Video rentals like the US, instead had neighbourhood uncles renting out latest DVDs? Or why Indian drivers are loath to wear seat belts but quickly bow when passing a roadside temple? And what does all this have to do with complicated economic theories? Read Sudipta Sarangi's delightful book to find out.'

—Ashwini Deshpande, professor of economics, Ashoka University

THE
ECONOMICS
OF
SMALL
THINGS

SUDIPTA SARANGI

FOREWORD BY *KAUSHIK BASU*

PENGUIN BOOKS

An imprint of Penguin Random House

PENGUIN BOOKS

USA | Canada | UK | Ireland | Australia
New Zealand | India | South Africa | China | Singapore

Penguin Books is part of the Penguin Random House group of companies
whose addresses can be found at global.penguinrandomhouse.com

Published by Penguin Random House India Pvt. Ltd
4th Floor, Capital Tower 1, MG Road,
Gurugram 122 002, Haryana, India

Penguin
Random House
India

First published in Penguin Books by Penguin Random House India 2020

Copyright © Sudipta Sarangi 2020
Foreword copyright © Kaushik Basu 2020

All rights reserved

10 9 8 7 6 5 4 3 2

The views and opinions expressed in this book are the author's own and the
facts are as reported by him which have been verified to the extent possible,
and the publishers are not in any way liable for the same.

ISBN 9780143450375

For sale in the Indian Subcontinent only

Typeset in Adobe Garamond Pro by Manipal Technologies Limited, Manipal

Printed at Manipal Technologies Limited, India

www.penguin.co.in

MIX
Paper | Supporting
responsible forestry
FSC® C043100

This is a legitimate digitally printed version of the book and therefore might not
have certain extra finishing on the cover.

For my parents,
Chandraparva and Arabinda Sarangi

Contents

Acknowledgements   ix
Foreword by Kaushik Basu   xiii
Introduction   xvii

1. All for One and One for All   1
2. The Economics of Video Rentals   11
3. Where Have All the Other Mangoes Gone?   21
4. In God We Trust   29
5. How About an MP from New Jersey?   37
6. Lessons from Stolen Shoes   45
7. Résumés or Cereals—Packaging Matters   53
8. A Tale of Two Bounties   61
9. Why We Should Pay Our Domestic Help More   71
10. Where the Mind Does Not Work   79
11. Pens in Pockets   87
12. Telegram. An Obituary. Stop   97
13. Rereading an Old Gandhi Essay   105

14. The Many Shades of Prejudice: A Look at
    the US and India   113

15. Capturing Indian 'Crab' Behaviour   123

16. Earthquake Economics   131

17. Palaces, Raki and Game Theory   141

18. Facebook against Corruption   151

19. Chicken: The Game Politicians Love to Play   159

20. The First Piece of Cake . . .   177

21. The Last Piece of Cake . . .   187

22. For a Few Overs More   199

23. Are More Choices Really Better?   211

24. P.G. Wodehouse, Futurist?   223

25. In Freedom Begins Responsibilities   229

Coda   241
Suggested Readings   249

Acknowledgements

As with most of my endeavours, I have benefited from encouragement, suggestions and criticisms offered by a large number of people from all walks of life. The limitations of my memory are responsible for this not-so-exhaustive list of people.

First, I need to thank Harish Damodaran, close friend and confidant with faith in my writing ability. During his time at *The Hindu BusinessLine*, Harish encouraged me to try popular writing and published my first piece 'P.G. Wodehouse, Futurist'. That was the beginning of this journey. I also need to thank Chandan Jha, my former PhD student who provided great research assistance and co-wrote *The Hindu BusinessLine* versions of several of the pieces included in this collection. Without him to ease the pressure, I would have given up writing such pieces early on.

Second, I need to thank Professor Kaushik Basu who has not only been a teacher par excellence and a great source of inspiration, but without his insistence, I would never have attempted to try my hand at writing a book. I will remain forever indebted to him for that.

I studied at the Ispat (E.M.) School in Rourkela and I am grateful for all the wonderful teachers we had—especially Meera Pradhan, Josephine Aquilla, Satwant Misra, Eric D'Costa and Srinath Bhanja. They inculcated in me a love for writing and helped me nurture it. Some of them have passed on now, but I am sure they would have been very proud of my book. And I would have loved to share it with them.

Over the years, many people have contributed to my education in economics which was the complementary skill needed for the completion of this book. In particular, I learned a lot from my teachers Shailaja Fennell, K. Narayanan and Jaivir Singh in Kirori Mal College. Professors V. Bhaskar and Kaushik Basu were the best mentors one could have asked for at the Delhi School of Economics and were always very supportive. As a PhD student, I learned about the importance of writing in economics, and both my doctoral supervisors, Hans Haller and Robert Gilles, played a very important role in this. Finally, just recently, I have started to teach a class called Economic Puzzles in History, Literature and Movies. The students in this class as well as my co-instructor Richard Cothren raised a number of thought-provoking questions that have helped with this book. Richard, in particular, has provided me all sorts of additional readings and anecdotes relevant to the material in the book as has my colleague Rick Ashley. My dean, Sally Morton, has always encouraged me to keep up my academic side even in the face of significant administrative tasks. Guru Ghosh has helped immensely by facilitating trips to India and providing stimulating conversations.

A large number of friends and colleagues have also participated in this endeavour and I could not list them all in any reasonable amount of space. However, some have made specific contributions to the book. Former students Bibhudutta Panda and Colin Cannonier were co-authors on *The Hindu BusinessLine* version of the cricket chapter, 'For a Few Overs More'. Similarly, Matt Wiser, also a former student, helped write one version of the 'Chicken' chapter. The chapter on efficiency wages, 'Why We Should Pay Our Maid More', was a direct consequence of discussions with my friend Arjya Chakravarty. Dr Ram Devireddy, who is the most erudite mechanical engineer I know, has provided very specific comments and they have always been great. Niloy Bose, friend and colleague, has patiently listened to me rave and rant about many of these ideas and has provided encouragement and libations throughout the process. My friends and co-authors Christophe Bravard and Pascal Billand have always been excellent at questioning the logic put forth in some of my pieces. It has helped me improve the clarity of my writing immensely. My technically non-economist friends Jagan Battu, Surajit Borkotokey, Diganta Mukherjee, Narayan Partangel and K.S. Mallikarajuna Rao have commented and inspired many bits and pieces of this book. My economist friends Subha Mani, Utteeyo Dasgupta and Saumyajit Bhattacharya, who are always interested in all things Indian, have provided astute observations about some of the more inscrutable parts in the book. Current students, Abhinaba Nandy and Ross Spoon, have provided excellent research assistance.

The editorial team at Penguin has really helped me understand how to write better and in the process has helped create a much better manuscript. My editors Paloma Dutta and Shreya Punj (as well Anushree Kaushal initially), of course, have provided wonderful feedback and motivation to keep pushing on.

Many members of the family have helped me by reading portions and providing suggestions and encouragement all along. My niece Dr Arundhati Acharya (and I think some of her friends as well) have provided feedback on many different aspects of the book. My brother Subrat Sarangi has been an excellent sounding board and my sister Sharmistha Sarangi an excellent listener and critic. My in-laws, Yashodhara and Satyananda Mishra, have provided encouragement, suggestions as well as information about the world of publishing. My brother-in-law Pallav Mishra also acted as a guinea pig for early drafts of some of the pieces.

My wife Sulagna Mishra has always provided outside-the-box insights on my writing. My daughter Amrita has been the source of several interesting conversations as well as the starting point for the piece on eating cake. I am very thankful to both of them for being patient with me and for the freedom they have given me to focus on my writing.

Finally, my biggest gratitude is to my parents who inculcated in me a love of reading and writing. Despite the fact that in the beginning I tried my best to resist their efforts, they never gave up. Without their patience and those teachers in my school, I would probably still be writing academic papers in economics but would never have written a book like this. My parents have always given me the freedom to pursue my passion and have supported me throughout my journey.

Foreword

Economists are generally preoccupied with big questions— a nation's economic growth, sustainable development, recessions, inflations, job gains and job losses. Perhaps that is how it should be; those are concerns with major implications for society and human well-being. But economics as a discipline also impinges on and interacts with our everyday lives, in ways that we are unaware of most of the time. Many of the social norms and cultural practices of societies across the world that evolved over the years are such a part and parcel of life that we are not conscious of their existence. Yet many of these norms and institutions play a crucial role in making our economy viable. And, further, the laws of economics and the struggle to make ends meet over hundreds and even thousands of years have left their mark on these norms and habits, as on a palimpsest. Evolution and the fact that we are still around ensures that.

The way to be aware of these social mores is not by the methods of normal economics, using mathematical models and statistical information, but by looking and studying our everyday lives with an outsider's objectivity. That is what

Sudipta Sarangi's wonderful little book, *The Economics of Small Things*, does. Drawing on examples from the dailiness of life, from snippets of history, from cinema, from gazing at the lives of people while travelling in unfamiliar places, Professor Sarangi does what economists rarely do, provides us with tales and analysis of everyday economics. He dips into some of the usual resources of the discipline for his analysis—the laws of demand and supply, methods of strategic choice, game theory, the meaning of knowing, and knowing or not knowing that one knows, and so on—and ends up with a delightful book for the specialist and layperson alike.

What makes reading this book unusual is how much one learns without being made aware that one is learning. It ranges over a host of important phenomena with a light touch. Thus we are enlightened about the path-breaking work by Muhammad Yunus in starting Grameen Bank and its use of subtle principles of economics, like peer monitoring, moral hazard and joint liability. We read about important contemporary matters such as how people protest in the age of social media, how people bond together when they face a common threat, etc. In these pages, we encounter important ideas like John Nash's concept of equilibrium, Thomas Schelling's idea of the focal point, and the role of beliefs of ordinary people in shaping our lives and laws.

Reading the book brought back to me memories from many years ago, when I was based in Delhi and taught at the Delhi School of Economics, where Sudipta was then a master's student. Because he lived in my neighbourhood in east Delhi, I would occasionally give him a ride in my car. While driving, we would chat—Sudipta, my wife and I—over the long, roughly forty-five-minute drive, out of Delhi University campus, past the sprawling inter-state bus terminus, up along Ring Road and over the Yamuna bridge. We would chat about economics, society, politics and Delhi School gossip. I recall how the subject of the economics of small things, in which I myself had an early interest, cropped up every now and then, such as, how not to lose one's footwear outside Indian temples. Earlier you had to leave your shoes outside, usually without any guard in attendance, in order to go into the temple premises. I had devised a method, which I had shared with family, friends and students. The method was to leave one shoe outside one entrance of the temple, hobble over to another entrance, and leave the other one there. By a simple reference to the complementarity of shoes, and the rationality of thieves with limited time on their hands, one could be fairly sure one's shoes would not be stolen. Friends who tried the same safety measure assured me it worked well.

Sudipta too talked about the economics of small things during those long drives. I do not recall the exact details of those conversations but remember the fact that they were fascinating conversations. I know he teaches a popular course at Virginia Tech titled 'Economic Puzzles in History, Literature and Movies'. I am sure some of the topics of this book figure in that course.

Reading the book, with its light-hearted tales, humorous episodes and economic analysis, I felt glad that Sudipta Sarangi decided to write a book on economics and the small things of life. Those who could not overhear the conversations during those long drives in Delhi, and those who are not able to attend his course at Virginia Tech, can now read the book and enjoy.

Kaushik Basu
Carl Marks Professor of International Studies,
Cornell University, New York
Former Chief Economist, World Bank, Washington

Introduction

6.53 a.m., Dibrugarh: Prof. Borkotokey switched off the alarm on his phone. He had already enjoyed 'one snooze' and now it was time to get up. In a few minutes he would be pouring that golden brown liquid into a fine bone china cup. That comforting thought always helped him get out of bed! A few minutes of scanning the newspaper and a couple of sips later, his brow creased up and there was a thoughtful look on his face. He turned to his wife and with a lot of feeling remarked that it was no longer possible to get great tea in Assam. She concurred and very matter-of-factly added that the best tea is exported anyway. Why did this happen, they wondered—it is not like the locals did not appreciate good tea. They in fact knew a number of people who enjoyed good tea but faced the same problem. But then, they both expressed relief that they had Marie biscuit, at least! Imagine drinking tea without Marie biscuit—that would just be the last straw. After going through the sports page, Prof. Borkotokey put aside the newspaper to look at his email on the phone. As he scanned through the new mails quickly, a smile broke out on his face—his paper had been accepted at the

Annals of Operations Research. He became completely absorbed in that email and suddenly nothing else mattered.

Breakfast: Mr Quereshi loved food. He sat down at the breakfast table and stared glumly at the steaming bowl in front of him—today was an oats day. This healthy breakfast was a far cry from his usual kachoris and piping hot jalebis. He was not averse to a nutritious first meal except on days like this. In general, when it came to sacrificing taste for health, he liked his masala oats—they were tasty and there was quite a bit of variety. He did not like all the flavours though, especially not the one on his plate today. With a deep sigh he launched himself into the task at hand wondering why there were so many varieties of masala oats, and why they made flavours that he did not like.

8.37 a.m., Mumbai: Prof. Rao was getting ready to walk down from his house to the institute department. Everything else done, he approached his desk, picked up his favourite fountain pen and stuck it in his shirt pocket; it was an old habit—he never left home without it. Of course, many people, including his wife, often wondered why he always carried a pen in his pocket in the age of smart devices. Today he was going to introduce game theory to the class, starting with simple games like Tic-Tac-Toe, and teaching them to think strategically—put yourself in the other person's shoes and anticipate what they would do, how you would respond to their action, and what would be their reaction in turn, and so on . . . It was going to be a fun class. It was almost time for class and the story of the pen in his pocket would have to wait for another day!

9.16 a.m., Chennai: Mr Sen was rushing down the stairs. He was already late for work and once again regretting the decision to binge-watch his favourite show on a Thursday night. His driver was waiting for him in the car. They would most definitely hit peak-hour traffic! Soon they were passing that famous Chennai temple and once again his driver, who never wore his seat belt while driving, said a quick prayer for safety. This daily ritual never failed to annoy Mr Sen. He was a confirmed atheist and could not endorse such behaviour. Unfortunately, before he could launch into a tirade, the phone rang—it was his wife. She had called to remind him to make an urgent bill payment if he wanted to avoid a late fee. He had a packed schedule today and realized that he would either have to make the payment immediately or accept the late fee. By the time he finished deliberating over this decision, they had already crossed the temple and Mr Sen discovered that he had again lost the opportunity to lecture his driver on the seat belt issue.

10.24 a.m., Rourkela: Mr D'Costa was walking to his class and looking forward to it, especially today, since they would start to study photosynthesis and the carbon cycle. In general, he was a good teacher and he looked forward to his classes every day. Once, one of his students had offered him an interesting argument: since Mr D'Costa explained things so well in class and made difficult concepts seem extremely easy, his students did not work as hard as they did in their other classes. In fact, the student had gone on to partially blame Mr D'Costa for his poor performance. An excellent example of 'moral hazard'—but what could he do? Become a bad teacher?

11.15 a.m., Gurgaon: Mrs Chakraborty stepped out of the car knowing fully well that Sheila would already be there at the bank—she understood the importance of being punctual. It was often said that poor people suffered because they did not have education and did stupid things routinely. Mrs Chakraborty knew that this was not true of Sheila—she usually made sensible decisions. When she did make poor choices, it was often because she was already distracted by some other worry. This trust was why she had agreed to be a co-signer for Sheila's loan. She knew Sheila would never default. In fact, she actually paid Sheila more than her other employees because she did not want to lose her. She had learned early on that it was best to hang on to a good thing!

Lunch: Jha ji watched that last piece of pizza steadfastly. It was always the same story: whenever they ordered pizza at work, everyone would pass up the last slice saying that they were completely full! Yet he knew very well that some of them— like Manas and Tarun, for example (he had seen them eating at buffets and knew their ravenous appetites only too well)—were simply pretending to not be hungry. Although he was also a willing participant, he never quite understood this silly farce. In the end, with a twinkle in her eye, Mrs Khanna would always brazenly grab the last slice of the pie. But today she was on leave and he wondered what fate had in store for that last piece . . .

Many more such quotidian stories could be told about people going through their daily businesses and, quite likely, some of these narratives will resonate with different readers. I could even find little episodes from *One Day in the Life of Ivan Denisovich* in his prison camp. In fact, these events could be set in different places, at different times, and be about people from various walks of life. There is one common thread running through them all, though—you can find serious economic behaviours in these snippets of life. And, in fact, you can read the book in any order you like, except may be for the 'cake' chapters.

This is a book about the economics of these small things. Over the course of the book, I will delve into the economic concepts behind the events mentioned here and other such phenomena drawn from everyday life. The book invites you to explore these different economic ideas and concepts—and to have fun while doing it. And for those interested in exploring these topics further, there is a detailed reading list at the end.

Happy reading!

All for One and One for All

At some stage in our lives all of us have had to work in groups—to either satisfy the whims of a teacher who wanted a group project or a boss who assigned a task to a team. On top of that, we often did not have the liberty to choose the members of the group and, quite possibly, if it was a boss doing the selection, not the task either; teachers in general are more accommodating than bosses. Consequently, we have all had a taste of that one person whom economists like to call 'the free-rider';[1] in this case, literally free-loading on the efforts of others who might have spent sleepless nights, or earned a few more grey hairs (I am not ruling out the possibility that the reader might have been the perpetrator in some cases). I am thinking of that person who would either not do the task assigned to them, or do it sloppily, or not show up for meetings, be late or fail to meet the deadline, etc. Thus, in general, getting groups to accomplish a set of goals is a difficult task.

---

[1] A free-rider is a person who consumes more than their fair share of a good, either by paying less than what they ought to or nothing at all. In the group project, the free-rider enjoys the credit earned by the entire group without incurring the necessary costs. Hence the name free-rider.

The Brilliance of Muhammad Yunus

And yet Muhammad Yunus, who was awarded the Nobel Prize for Peace in 2006, came up with an idea that involved lending to a group. Not only was it an immensely successful lending programme, it was able to go where no formal lending programme had gone before—it was able to lend to the poor! Formal banking institutions never want to lend to the poor because in the absence of a credit score or the ability to verify their incomes in a credible manner, it is prohibitively expensive to assess the creditworthiness of a *poor borrower* interested in a *small sum* of money. It does not help that the impoverished also have no collateral to speak of. Thus before the arrival of the type of lending programmes pioneered by Mr Yunus, their only option was the village moneylender, or the *sahukar*, like in the Hindi movies of the sixties.

While working as an economics professor at Dhaka University, Professor Yunus realized that having access to small sums of money could significantly improve the lives of the poor, and yet no such loans were available to them. He decided that he would arrange for small loans to be given to groups of poor borrowers under certain conditions. First, the loan would be given only to a group. Second, the group would be jointly liable for the entire loan of the group, giving a new meaning to the Three Musketeers' motto, 'One for all and all for one.' Third, the bank would not assign potential borrowers into a group. The groups had to be formed endogenously, i.e., members of a group must find each other and come to the bank together for a loan. There were also other rules like members could not be blood relatives, etc. But these were the key facts that helped Prof. Yunus overcome what economists call the unholy trinity of asymmetric information—adverse selection, moral hazard and costly state verification.

Asymmetric Information

A situation involving two parties is said to have asymmetric information when both parties may not be fully informed about each other. Common instances of one-sided asymmetric information are when, for instance, the lender may not know the borrower's ability to repay a loan or when a firm selling health insurance may not know the buyer's state of health. Information asymmetry can also be two-sided: imagine you move to a new town and are looking for a place to continue your martial arts education. Obviously, you do not know which the best training academy for your needs is. Similarly, a martial arts academy might prefer a certain type of student only—for instance, someone who is very disciplined—and they do not know if you satisfy this criteria. This is a simple example of two-sided asymmetric information.

So what was the operating procedure of Professor Yunus's lending programme?

If you needed to borrow money, you would have to find a friend (the formal operation founded by Muhammad Yunus is called the Grameen Bank and requires a group size of five members) who also wanted to borrow money.[2] Then you would each ask the bank for a loan, and if the bank gave Rs 10,000

---

[2] It is believed that the Grameen Bank arrived at the number five by experimenting with different group sizes. If the group was too small, then the joint liability would not have bite, and if it was too large, then it would be unmanageable for the borrowers.

per head, then you would both be responsible for paying the total loan amount of Rs 20,000. We can now understand why Professor Yunus's idea was so effective in solving the asymmetric-information problems involved in lending to the poor and why it has been emulated repeatedly all over the world.[3]

The Problem of Adverse Selection

A serious consequence of asymmetric information is adverse selection.[4] We know that it would be too expensive for a bank to find

---

[3] Although it is not exactly related, I love this quote from Muhammad Yunus's book that he has co-authored with Carl Weber, *Creating a World without Poverty: Social Business and the Future of Capitalism* (2009): 'To me, the poor are like bonsai trees. When you plant the best seed of the tallest tree in a six-inch-deep flower pot, you get a perfect replica of the tallest tree, but it is only inches tall. There is nothing wrong with the seed you planted; only the soil-base you provided was inadequate. Poor people are bonsai people. There is nothing wrong with their seeds. Only society never gave them a base to grow on.'

[4] Adverse selection occurs when one party in a transaction has (relevant) information that the other party lacks. This leads to certain types of informed participants dominating the market. Consider the issue of buying health insurance. Clearly, the buyers are better informed about how sick they are. So when the insurance company offers an insurance plan, only those who are less healthy will buy the insurance. Thus, to make profits, the insurance company will have to raise the price of the insurance plan. However, at the new (higher) price, some of the less-healthy people who were willing to purchase insurance earlier will drop out, and only the really unhealthy will buy insurance. This will set off a vicious cycle where the insurance mechanism will select the group that affects things adversely, as opposed to the group that would be favoured by 'natural selection'.

out the creditworthiness of every borrower in a village interested in a loan for only Rs 10,000, i.e., given the small amount, cost of disbursing the loan would be very high in relation to any potential profits. Moreover, if the bank offers the loan at too low a rate of interest, it will attract both safe and risky borrowers. Therefore the bank has to raise the interest rate on its loan. However, at a higher interest, some of the safe borrowers might not want to borrow any more, leaving a larger pool of risky borrowers in the market. This is also why when you go looking for a used car, you are more likely to find a 'lemon'. The bank will now need to raise the price of the loan, i.e., the interest rate, to accommodate the even riskier business prospects leading to a vicious circle of upward spiralling interest rates and a larger fraction of risky borrowers. Alternatively, unless the insurance company can do background checks, only the sick will demand medical insurance, i.e, we will see the adverse selection of the sickly into health insurance.

However, if you are responsible for your partner's loan and have the option to choose your partner, it is unlikely that you will choose a risky partner. Since your partner will also follow the same reasoning, and forming a group will require *mutual consent*, only safe groups will be formed. And in this manner, lending to a jointly liable group overcomes adverse selection, leading to the high repayment rates observed for the Grameen Bank and other such group-lending programmes.

The Problem of Moral Hazard

Imagine that you have no collateral and the bank cannot seize your assets (since you have none), it is possible that you may not put all your effort into working hard. You might even take the money and try to flee the country! If you did have something to protect, you might want to work hard. This situation where an individual puts in less than the optimal effort is termed a 'moral hazard problem' by economists.[5] For instance, a driver who has auto insurance might drive more rashly than one without such insurance because they have nothing to protect them.

When you are responsible for your partner's loan, you will make sure that your partner puts in the optimal effort and does not take unnecessary risks. They will also ensure that you put in the optimal effort and not engage in unnecessary risk-taking, thereby vanquishing the moral-hazard demon.

The Problem of Costly State-Verification

It is easy to see the costly state-verification problem.[6] Since the borrower has nothing (like collateral or credit rating) to lose, in spite of making a profit, a borrower might report losses to the bank and an inability to repay the loan. Unfortunately, for a loan of Rs 10,000, a bank will not send an individual to the

---

[5] Moral hazard occurs when a person takes risks simply because they do not have to face the consequences of this risk-taking. The classic example, as explained in the chapter 'In God We Trust', is that when seat belts were introduced, the number of accidents remained unchanged but pedestrian casualties increased. The story goes as follows: drivers felt safe wearing seat belts, became rasher drivers and the consequences of this were borne by pedestrians. Thus the term moral hazard.

[6] As the name suggests, it is costly (usually for the lender) to verify the performance or the output of one of the parties (usually the borrower) in a transaction. It is not without reason that in certain types of small businesses, like the restaurant business, there is a tendency to employ family members only, at least in management roles. This eliminates the need for worrying about the manager raiding the till.

village to verify the borrower's state, that is, check whether they incurred profits or losses.

However, your partner who lives in the village would know about your profits or losses, and would certainly make every effort to find out the true state of your performance, since they are also responsible for your loan. Thus the problem of costly state verification is solved.

It is easy to see why the Grameen Bank model works: banks may not know whether people are safe or risky borrowers, whether borrowers will work hard or not and whether they made profits or losses. However, people in a group being from the same village will have access to all this knowledge, meaning that they do not dwell in the world of asymmetric information. Since they are jointly responsible for the loan, they will choose the right group, avoid unnecessary risk, put in the required effort and not lie about the outcome. Thus loans will be repaid, banks will be in business and the poor can have access to credit.

How Did Mr Sahukar Do It?

The sahukar had a whole bag of tricks which enabled him to operate successfully as a moneylender to the poor. First, he lived in the same village. So he was certainly better informed about the economic situation of his borrowers. Second, he had the ubiquitous *munshiji*, aka Jeevan,[7] who knew everything that was

---

[7]   Onkar Nath Dhar, aka Jeevan, was born in Srinagar in 1915, educated in Lahore and came to Bombay at the age of eighteen to try his hand in the movies. He was the quintessential scheming munshiji, though his claim to fame is that he is supposed to have portrayed Narad Muni forty-nine times. He passed away in 1987 at the age of seventy-one.

there to know about everybody, the information often going back generations. Then, of course, the sahukar also had a coterie of thugs who could solve any costly state-verification problem. His last resort has been the plot of numerous Hindi movies— if all else failed, he could force the borrower into indentured labour, imposing insufferable misery on the borrower and his family. Sometimes two brothers would get separated because of this. At other times, the sahukar would covet the borrower's daughter in marriage providing the hero of the movie his arch nemesis and a chance to rid the village of evil.

Written on an Air France flight en route from Paris to Washington DC after reading a short piece on Alexandre Dumas's The Three Musketeers.

The Economics of Video Rentals

Although the downward spiral had been going on for some time, the end finally came in November 2013: video-rental giant Blockbuster LLC announced the closure of its last store in the US, marking the demise of yet another industry, hastened by technological advancement. For those of you who have grown up in the era of streaming services, the name of this rental service probably means nothing. But plenty of folks who did their graduate studies in the US in the nineties, including me, and others of a certain age all over the world, will fondly remember the weekend video-store run to pick up new movies that had just been released on DVD. It was affordable entertainment, and I have many fond memories of those days.

Rapid advances in streaming technology have given rise to a whole new set of firms like Netflix, Hulu and Amazon Video providing instant access to movies. These media service providers, with the help of new technology, eliminated the need to go to a store to rent a movie and then again to return it. This small convenience made possible by technological advances essentially killed the video-rental business.[1] But sometimes even the dead

---

[1] It also killed the big one-screen, one-movie theatres. Their new avatar is the multiplexes, which is not a one-movie theatre, but a number of screens simultaneously offering a whole range of movies, though each theatre has a somewhat smaller capacity. Similarly, recall

can tell tales and I want to use this occasion to reflect on the lessons in economics that one might learn from the extinct physical video-rental industry. But first I want to take a trip down memory lane and start at the very beginning, briefly covering how the experience of watching movies itself has evolved over time.

Technology and the Viewing Experience

In India, in the beginning, there was only one channel—Doordarshan, the national broadcaster. If you had a TV, you watched whatever movie Doordarshan chose for you, typically on the weekends. If it was age-appropriate, the whole family watched the movie together, and sometimes the neighbours without TVs joined in. The most significant consequence of this was that the next day everyone had one common thing to talk about. Today this is possible only after an exciting cricket match. Then in the early eighties technology brought us a new device called the video cassette recorder (VCR). For the first time you could plug a device into your TV and play a video cassette to watch a movie. It was expensive and only the rich owned a unit. More commonly, families would pool money together and rent out a VCR along with a bunch of movie cassettes and make a night of entertainment of it. It was the original form of binge-watching—you had to get your rupee's worth from renting the VCR. However, the next morning, since different people watched different movies,

---

how Ayushmann Khurrana's (screen name Prem Prakash Tiwari) audio-cassette store was threatened by a new store selling CDs in the thoroughly enjoyable movie *Dum Laga Ke Haisha*. In short, technological progress has always had a disrupting influence on the entertainment industry.

there no longer was a single topic of conversation. But it did bring people together and invented binge-watching. By the late nineties, the VCR got replaced by the digital video disc (DVD) player. Moreover, unlike the VCR, the cost of the DVD player fell rather quickly and people began owning their own DVD players. Since we all prefer watching movies from the comfort of our own home with our own favourite snacks, gradually, the group-watching experience of the eighties died out along with all the fun, the shared dishes, the stolen glances and the conspiratorial conversations associated with such social events. Finally, in recent years, we have the streaming services which offer the variety of the DVD, but now, even within a family, everyone can watch a different show simultaneously on their personal devices. This, however, rids even a family unit of a common source of entertainment to discuss the next morning.

Bolly versus Holly

Some decades ago, the above story of ownership and the use of devices was similar, at least in urban areas, in India and the US. Back then, consumers in India lagged behind their American counterparts in terms of technology and the variety of shows they had access to by a few years at the most—today, the gap might be less than a few months. However, when it came to the marketing and distribution of video cassettes or DVDs, the story panned out quite differently in the two countries. In the US, most video cassettes or DVDs were available on rent from a few national chains. Mom-and-pop stores were the exception, largely catering to niche markets like off-beat movies, foreign flicks or simply good old porn. But none of these rentals offered pirated movies. In India, by contrast, small stores were the norm. The ubiquitous neighbourhood 'video parlour' stocked the entire gamut of movies to satisfy all tastes, including pirated copies of the latest releases.

So, why this difference?

One reason, of course, was the stringent intellectual property protection laws and their equally strong enforcement in the US. But the structure of the market also played an important role. In the US, large video-rental firms—the likes of Blockbuster—had the means to strike deals with Hollywood studios and film distributors, to acquire the official versions of movies. On the other hand, the corner video-store guy in India did not have the wherewithal to negotiate with distributors and movie studios. The typical video-store owner in India was just like Ajay Devgn in *Drishyam*. Can you imagine the lead character of Vijay Salgaonkar, the owner of Mirage Cable Network (Ajay Devgn in the movie), negotiating with Yash Raj Studios for copies of their latest blockbuster? But given our lax intellectual property laws, he can earn enough by coolly renting out pirated versions of those same movies. The message here seems to be that the existence of enforceable property rights in the US spurred the growth of a market dominated by a few large firms, which simultaneously curbed piracy. In other words, big can sometimes be beautiful—at least from the perspective of movie producers and firms, big and small.

Sorting Out Consumers

Next, let's consider another interesting aspect in which video-rental markets differed in the two countries. In India, your typical video-store owner was just like the character of Vijay Salgaonkar in *Drishyam*: you knew him, and he knew you and your taste in movies quite well. In this personalized world of informal transactions, you rarely paid a late fee. In the US, however, video-rental stores thrived on the dreaded late fee. In fact, they often made a third of their revenues from late fees alone. Moreover, the late fee was a boon in another way. It provided a means to sort the consumers into different groups, thereby allowing the seller to engage in the practice of *price discrimination*, or charging different prices to different segments of the market for the very same product.

Here is how it works.

When a firm charges one price to all consumers, some end up paying less than what they would have been *willing to pay* for that good. This difference between what they are willing to pay and what they actually pay (the price) is called 'consumer's surplus'.[2] While benefiting the consumer by allowing them to consume the product at a price less than or equal to what they would be willing to pay, the goal of a firm is to appropriate as much of surplus as possible.[3] So if a bottle of water is being sold

---

[2] Remember Nawazuddin Siddiqui's (Rafi in the movie) quest for Campa Cola in the movie *Photograph* to make Sanya Malhotra (Miloni in the movie) happy. He was ready to pay any amount to find a bottle of Campa Cola. For the sake of argument, let us say that he was willing to pay Rs 1000 for a bottle. If someone would have sold him a bottle for Rs 436, then his consumer's surplus is 1000-436 = Rs 564. However, in the movie, Sam Kerawalla (Mr Sodabottlewallah in the movie) offers it to him for free and therefore his consumer's surplus is 1000-0 = Rs 1000.

[3] Similarly, the difference between what they charge (the price) and what the seller would have been willing to sell a product for is called the 'producer's surplus' or 'profit'. And now you can easily see what bargaining is all about. Buyers and sellers bargain about the difference between their willingness to pay and willingness to sell. By negotiating the price they are each trying to maximize their share. So imagine the seller was willing to sell the soda bottle to Rafi at a

at Rs 10, I am willing to bet that you are leaving the NRI with a considerable amount of consumer's surplus—their purchasing power would have allowed them to pay more considerably for that bottle. Therefore, an Indian firm would make more profits if it could charge the NRI a higher price than the Indian citizen.

But the problem is consumers don't walk into a store and declare the maximum that they would be willing to pay for the goods. Granted, in the case of the NRI, there may be some visible or audible signs! But this is not true in general. Hence, sellers need to find ways of making consumers sort themselves into different groups according to their willingness to pay on their own! This they do by selling different quantities (bulk discounts) or qualities (different classes of airline travel) at different prices, besides offering stuff such as discount coupons.

Late Fees

A late fee is normally viewed as a deterrence instrument—a punishment to ensure people return things on time. But let me argue that a firm can use late fees as an instrument for indirectly segmenting the market. Imagine two types of consumers—those who have very high value for their time (say, corporate executives) and those who assign lower value to their time, like college students drinking endless cups of tea and coffee. Also,

---

price of Rs 200. Then his producer's surplus is 436-200 = Rs 236. This is what bargaining is about. If on the other hand the negotiated price would have been Rs 600, the buyer and the seller would both have had a surplus of Rs 400 (600-200 for the seller and 1000-600 for the buyer) and the gains from trade would have been equally shared.

assume that both sets of consumers are aware of the *possibility* of something unexpected turning up, which might lead to their returning a video rental late and paying the associated penalty. Hence, it is reasonable to assume that everyone's aware of the probability of being late at the time of renting—though no one intends to be late!

Now since the clever video-store owner knows this, he could reduce the rental price. The lower price will, then, induce people to rent more videos. If the consumers include many executives who, being terribly busy, tend to forget, then the store could make a lot of money through late fees. The best strategy in this case would be to set a high late fee—much higher than the rental price of a video. This will, first of all, ensure that students who value money more than time would keep returning the videos on time so that the store's inventory is not substantially affected. They will also tend to rent more videos given its low rental (or base) price. Second, the stores will make a lot of money by charging the high late fees from corporate executives who are prone to returning late. Such a price scheme was, in fact, followed in the video industry in the late nineties. Some firms would charge late fees that were 60 per cent, or more, than the rental price. In such a scenario, if you are unable to watch the movie during the stipulated period and are willing to take the trouble of going to the store, you could avoid the late fee by re-renting at the lower rental price.

Needless to add, this strategy isn't restricted to just the video-rental industry. Research in the US[4] shows competing

---

[4] Nadia Massoud, Anthony Saunders and Barry Scholnick, 'The Cost of Being Late? The Case of Credit Card Penalty Fees', *Journal of Financial Stability* 7.2 (2011): 49–59.

credit card companies use similar strategies (by introducing a variety of fees but offering lower interest rates), and it probably holds for credit cards in India as well. I am also certain that there are readers who have been a part of such creative marketing strategies to extract more consumer's surplus from us buyers, even beyond the video-rental industry. And so while that industry may no longer be around, the lessons in economics it provided remain relevant for all times.

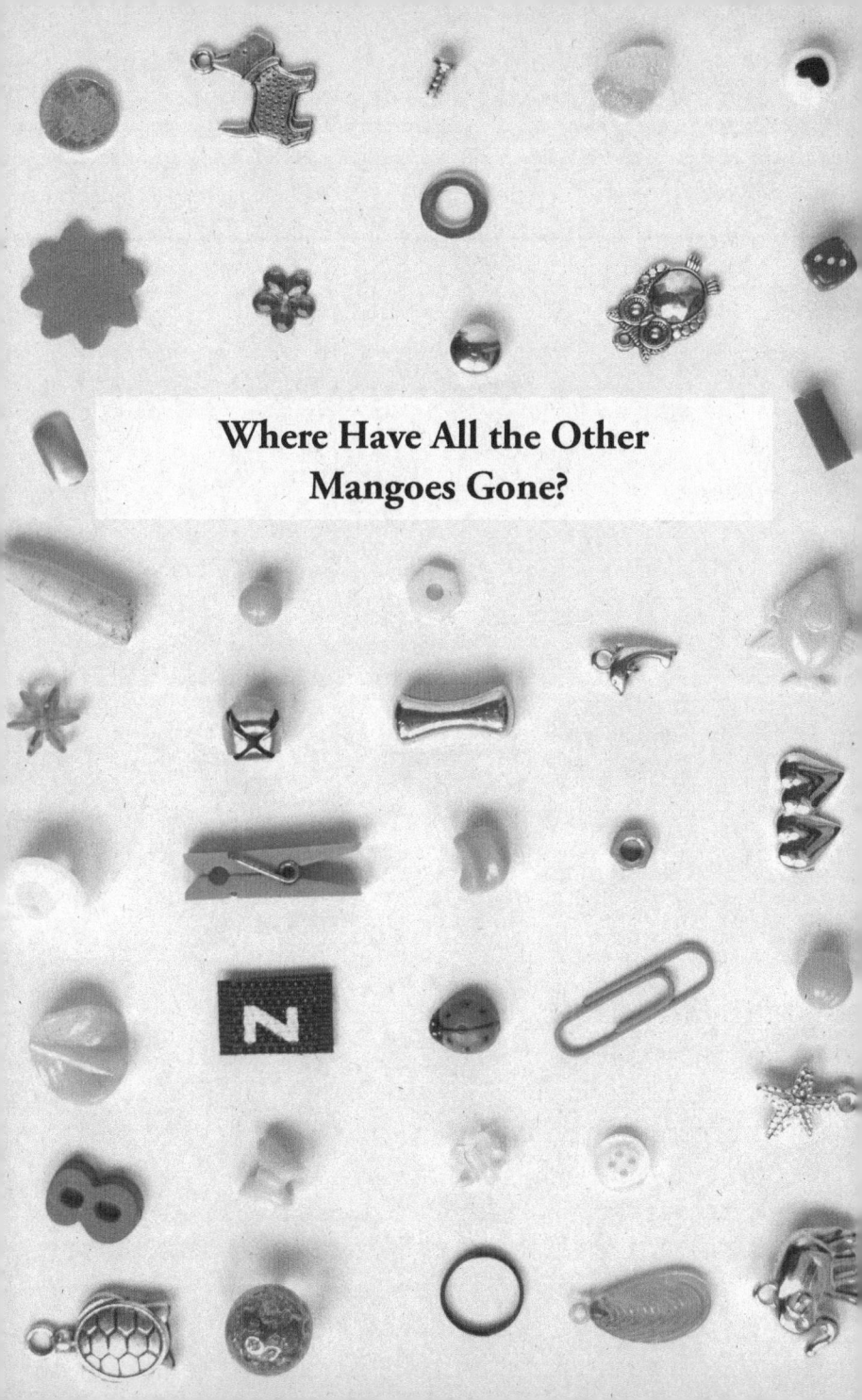

Where Have All the Other
Mangoes Gone?

Living in the US, one of the things you miss the most about India is the mango season—mangoes announce the arrival of summer. Their sweetness is the saving grace of our hot summer days and the season fades away only when the monsoons step in to provide the much-needed relief to the country. One sorely misses the myriad flavours, smells and tastes of the endless varieties of mangoes back home. Just the thought of sinking my teeth into a ripe mango, juice running down my chin and fingers, makes my mouth water!

Unfortunately, what pass as mangoes in the regular grocery stores here in America are offerings from South America. To me, and presumably my fellow non-resident Indians, these so-called mangoes, usually of Mexican or Peruvian origin, are flavourless and tasteless; they are simply big, nothing more. True, you also have the Indian and, to some extent, Asian and international grocery stores (interestingly called 'ethnic grocery stores' to differentiate from the regular grocery stores) where you'll most certainly find boxes of that king of mangoes—the Alphonso. But you won't see any other variety. In fact, a person wanting to draw conclusions about India from what the country exports will instantly conclude that India only produces a single variety of mangoes. When I ask these ethnic grocery-store owners here why they only have the Alphonso mangoes, their stock response is: 'Alphonso is the king of mangoes' and they only sell the best Indian mango. 'In any case, only the best things from all the countries in the world get sent to the US!' The final part of this piece of logic has always struck a chord with me because it matches with what I used to hear in India as a student: we send our 'best' products abroad and sell only the export rejects, or 'factory seconds', on the lanes of the famous Janpath market in Delhi. What never fails to amaze me is the fact that you hear the same answer regardless of whether you cross the seven seas or not.

The Third Law

Much as one dislikes this state of affairs, i.e., the lack of variety in mangoes in the US, it is quite often the case that the best products from any place are shipped out elsewhere. A simple economic explanation for this was put forth by Armen Alchian and William R. Allen in their classic 1967 textbook, *University Economics*. This phenomenon is sometimes referred to as the 'third law of demand'.

To understand it, assume that there are only two kinds of mangoes—high-quality (like our Alphonso) and low-quality (insert the name of your least favourite type of Indian mango). For the sake of simplicity, let's take the latter to cost Rs 30 per kg and the former Rs 300 per kg in India. A simple way to compare these two numbers is that 1 kg of high-quality mangoes is equivalent to 10 kg of low-quality mangoes. Next, suppose it costs Rs 60 to send a kilogram of mangoes, regardless of their quality, to the US. Taking this into account, a kilogram of high-quality mangoes will cost Rs 360 in the US, while it will cost Rs 90 for a kilogram of low-quality mangoes. Thus, in the US, a kilogram of high-quality mangoes works out to be the equivalent of only 4 kg of low-quality mangoes. Relatively speaking, then—when denominated in low-cost mangoes—high-quality mangoes are cheaper in the US than they are in India. It is natural, therefore, to expect American consumers to demand high-quality mangoes, since their cost measured in terms of low-cost mangoes is lower than what it is for consumers in India. In other words, American consumers feel that they buy Alphonsos at a bargain.

Keeping the above logic in mind, mango sellers will want to ship high-quality mangoes to the US. From this, it follows that the probability of finding high-quality mangoes is much higher in the US than in India. And once Alphonso has been branded the best mango, you'll see no other Indian variety in the US!

Some Caveats

Notice that these arguments rest on the fact that if we add the 'same fixed costs per kg' (which needn't just be transport charges and do not vary with the mango type, or with the number of kilos produced) to both high-quality and low-quality goods, the high-quality goods become relatively cheaper. Herein lies the first caveat—the fixed-costs amount needs to be more or less identical for our arguments to hold true. It is quite possible that the handling costs for low-quality mangoes may be significantly lower compared to that of high-quality ones. What matters is that the fixed costs do not have to be identical, but should not be substantially different between high-quality and low-quality mangoes.

Second, it is assumed that the entire fixed costs can be transferred to consumers. In our example, the price of both types of mangoes goes up by Rs 60, although this strict requirement is not really germane to our arguments. It can be less than Rs 60, but we will need to go through more hoops to make the point and that is not worth it for the sake of illustration. All that we really require is that the post-shipping price paid by the consumer makes the high-quality product relatively cheaper.

And third, we are only talking of mangoes being shipped out of India. Our example compares Alphonsos in India to selling them in the US. The fact that those 'mangoes' from South America can be substitutes for Alphonso mangoes or even our so-called low-quality mangoes (Rs 30 per kg, ex-India) isn't entering the calculations at all. Most Indians I know, though, would not really consider them substitutes!

The Travel Dimension

An interesting aspect of the third law of demand is that it holds even if the consumer has to travel instead of the good getting shipped to them. To illustrate this, we could consider an IPL match being played at the Barabati Stadium in Cuttack. First, suppose a resident of Cuttack and someone from the Steel City of Rourkela—where I did my entire schooling—are planning to watch this game. Now, suppose that the cost of travelling from Rourkela to Cuttack and back is Rs 1000 per person. Moreover, let us assume the price of a cheap Barabati Stadium ticket to be Rs 1000 and a premium one to be Rs 3000.

In this case, the *total cost* for our guy from Rourkela works out to be Rs 2000 (=1000+1000) for the cheap ticket, or Rs 4,000 (=1000+3000) for the premium experience. Effectively, one premium ticket for him is worth two cheap tickets (4000 vs 2000). But for the local Cuttack guy, one premium ticket can buy three cheap tickets (3000/1000). The relative cheapness of the premium ticket for the Rourkelaite makes it more likely for him to go for it than his counterpart from Cuttack. To see it another way—suppose bosom buddies Bunty and Dippy are planning to travel to Toronto and are weighing their ticket options. Bunty lives in Cuttack and his travel agent says that the business class ticket on Air Canada will cost three times as much as the economy class ticket. Dippy lives in Rourkela and his travel agent says that the business class ticket on Air Canada will only cost twice as much. Who do you think is more likely to feel that they are getting a deal and will therefore demand the business class ticket? Clearly, Dippy from Rourkela. To sum up, the third law of demand operates both ways—whether it is the good or the consumer that is travelling.

The First Two Laws

Well, what about the first two laws of demand? After all, they precede the third law. We all probably know the first law intuitively, at least through everyday experience. It states that ceteris paribus, or keeping everything else constant, the lower the price of a good, the higher the quantity demanded and vice versa. This is rather intuitive. Imagine that you are hungry and are in a restaurant that sells idlis. As you consume more idlis and feel fuller, each additional plate of idlis will give you less satisfaction. Consequently, you will only be willing to buy more idlis at a lower price, giving us a downward sloping demand curve. That 'keeping everything else constant' part—meaning income, tastes, prices of other goods, etc.—of the statement is, of course, crucial. This law may simply not hold when we relax the ceteris paribus assumption. For instance, when your income increases significantly, you will probably buy more of most goods at all prices.[1]

The second less-known law of demand states that a good is more responsive to changes in price in the long run than in the short run. Essentially, in the long run more substitutes can be found. It allows the quantities purchased to adjust more easily to prices. Thus, if the price of petrol increases by 50 per cent, you may not be able to find a flat close to your place of work overnight. But in the long run, you'll probably move closer to your workplace, which will enable you to consume a much lower quantity of petrol.

As the economist Eugene Silberberg, writing about the third law of demand, in a letter to the *Seattle Times* on 28 October 1975, put it so well, a simple explanation underlies most economic phenomena: 'It is no conspiracy—just the laws of supply and demand.'

---

[1] I say most goods because there are some things we purchase less of when our income increases. For example, when their income increases, most Indians consume less public transport. Such goods, whose demand declines when income increases, are called 'inferior goods'.

In God We Trust

Game theory is the study of any rule-governed situation, where the final outcome depends on the actions of more than one person. Sometimes, the same situation (game) can be experienced (played) over and over again by the same set of individuals. Repeated games, then, become the study of the finite or infinite repetition of a single or one-shot game. Imagine playing Rock-Paper-Scissors repeatedly or take the instance of a political party engaged in fighting elections in a constituency over the years. Alternatively, let us go back to the original question of economics—why are some countries rich while others are poor? This game of growth between countries, for example, may require, among other factors, accepting a certain level of industrial pollution for higher and faster growth. The time dimension is one aspect that makes the analysis of repeated games fundamentally different from the analysis of static or one-shot games. It requires us to think carefully about what we earn in a game today versus what we gain tomorrow, i.e., in terms of a country's development, we may achieve immediate higher growth but with the possibility of having to deal with more pollution in the future. Of course, different countries might pursue this strategy to a different extent, creating the possibility of different amounts of pollution. So, even if one country chooses green growth, some other country or countries might not follow suit. As a result, while some citizens may have a higher standard of living today, the next generation will quite likely have to deal with a more polluted earth in the future. Therefore, how much we care about today's utility (our immediate consumption) versus future utility (the consumption of our future generations) will certainly affect our decisions.

Another crucial aspect is the fact that the behaviour of players today—and, therefore, the outcome of the game—can influence responses tomorrow. For instance, if an incumbent firm wishes to deter entrants, that is, not allow new firms into its market, even if that decision comes at a huge cost, what it would be seeking is to build a reputation for being tough. So, the existing firm might lower the prices of its product in a particular market and even incur losses for an extended period, to signal to other firms that it is a tough player and will fight to the end.[2] Doing this once will then deter all future entry by potential market rivals. Such a position by a firm is called 'strategic reputation' and is an important part of the study of repeated games.

However, even 'non-strategic' or simple reputation, where an entity simply adopts some behaviour without any desire to exploit it in the future, can be very useful in explaining many types of observed behaviours. By now, you may be asking: why are we engaging in this droll excursion into the esoteric realm of repeated games? *'Toh mainuki'*, or 'Why should I care', to use that delectable Punjabi expression. *Well, because many of the seemingly irrational*

---

[2] This has interesting implications, especially when firms are heterogeneous. Imagine, for instance, a large retailer and a mom-and-pop store operating in a particular town. The large retailer can lower its price and sustain losses for a suitably long period to drive the mom-and-pop store out of business. Eventually, the large retailer becomes the sole seller, or monopolist, and can then charge a higher price without the fear of retaliation by a rival firm.

things that we do/observe can actually be explained using notions from repeated games.

Protecting God's Children

Many drivers in India will say a quick prayer while passing a temple and expect the reigning deity to protect them from mishaps on the road. These same drivers, however, will typically not wear a seat belt (a device guaranteed to provide greater protection in the event of an accident) let alone suggest this to their co-passengers—unless compelled by an external agent. Similarly, many private vehicle owners (including some in my family) will utter prayers to their respective gods even before starting their cars, and then drive off without wearing the seat belt.

Of course, many of these believers have started to wear seat belts now. But that's more from a fear of the law than safety for self. The task of keeping the occupants of the vehicle safe is still left in the hands of the Almighty. I shall now provide an argument based on repeated games to explain this behaviour and contend that similar arguments can be made for many other seemingly unreasonable acts. Although the act of depending on a prayer but not wearing a seat belt is not by any means ne plus ultra, it is still a perfect example for our purposes of illustration.

In the simplest version of our game, we have somebody making car trips daily. Recall, that a game is a rule-governed situation and it is therefore necessary to spell out all the rules at the beginning. This first player has four choices: (a) wear the seat belt and not pray; (b) pray, but not wear the seat belt; (c) do both; (d) do neither. Either way, we can assume the person's pay-off in the game to be maximized when they live longer.

The second player in our game is god, who can either choose to keep the first person safe or not. So, on the one hand, we have the Almighty in all his forms and manifestations—omnipotent, omnipresent and omniscient. He, indeed, pervades all spheres of the lives of us humble mortals.[3]

Player 3: The Mortal Seat Belt

And, let us not forget Player 3: the puny three-point seat belt— the brainchild of safety-minded engineers, who cannot aspire to any sort of godly status. The modern seat belt was patented in 1951 by Roger Griswold and Hugh de Haven, while the current three-point version, I understand from Wikipedia, is attributed to a Swedish mechanical engineer, Nils Ivar Bohlin, who worked for Volvo. The original seat belt was invented in the early nineteenth century by Sir George Cayley, also called the 'father of aerodynamics'. But it was a California neurologist, C. Hunter Sheldon, who—after undertaking numerous studies of head injuries—proposed the idea of retractable seat belts (along with other assorted safety improvements) to the automobile industry in the early 1950s. Needless to say, none of these versions have the potency of god. At best, seat belts are usually seen as irritants one has to put up with for avoiding a challan, or entering into a settlement with the traffic cop—a god no less.

Now, consider our Player 1, who does not wear the seat belt and prays to god before turning the ignition key each time. Every day that they make it back home safe, is a point

---

[3] It goes without saying that our first player, who exercises choice (b), strongly identifies with this supreme entity and has invested a lot of faith in him.

in favour of god, and with every passing day, god's reputation as the saviour grows. With that, so does the individual's trust in him, much like the reputation of an eBay or Amazon seller, who repeatedly delivers the products that you ask and pay for online. But unlike what happens on eBay or Amazon, a few near-fatal misses in this case may even serve to increase our first player's faith in god. The seat belt, as far as faith is concerned, by contrast, does not stand a chance!

Over time, the faith in god increases due to the repeated nature of this person's interaction with him, whereas the seat belt is remembered only when the supposedly long arm of the law forcefully rears its head. And thus, prayers are offered before starting any trip, and at every passing shrine, while the object specifically created to protect (the three-point seat belt) is treated as an irritant and religiously ignored.

Things would be different only if we could somehow deify the seat belt. What if among the Hindu pantheon of gods—33 crore is the most scholarly estimate—we also had a God of the Seat Belt?[4] Then, there might just be more takers for wearing their seat belts, just to appease him by another name. But then again, it might just be possible that people while riding cars may target their prayers to its God, while never actually wearing the seat belt.

That would become another repeated game, where safety once again would be relegated to the gods in whom we trust more than just safety mechanisms.

---

[4] Or for that matter, the God of Red Lights for the instances when we run a red light. Though, given the number of two-wheeler accidents in India every year, what we really need is a God of Motorcycle Helmets.

How About an MP from New Jersey?

While passing through France in the summer of 2012, I learned that London would have its own member of Parliament (MP) in the French Parliament. This bit of information was more than a little surprising to me. It is true that quite a few countries allow their citizens living abroad to vote. But a move like this seemed to be stepping things up a notch: Expats would not only be able to vote, but they would also have their 'own' voice in Parliament, *with their place of residence itself becoming a constituency.* To put it in terms Francis Bacon would—if the mountain will not come to Muhammad, then Muhammad must go to the mountain. The idea was certainly novel for me.

It turns out that London could be construed as the sixth-largest French city in terms of population. There are apparently 3,00,000 to 4,00,000 French citizens living in London, of whom about 1,20,000 are registered with the consulate, thus enabling them to vote—which they actually did sometime in June 2012. After a little research, I found out that it is not London per se that is getting an MP in the French Parliament. The constituency itself is called Northern Europe, covering a staggering geographical area of 4 million sq. km. That's bigger than even Rajasthan, which stretches a little over 342 thousand sq. km. Imagine, campaigning over this territory! However, that would still be child's play compared to the task facing those who wish to win the Asia (including Russia), Oceania or the Central and South American constituencies. There are actually eleven MPs in all, representing the French living in different parts of the world based on the registered French population in these countries. The easier constituencies, in that sense, would be Benelux, Switzerland and Liechtenstein.

Gaining Ground

However, it is not the French who started this practice. Italy passed a law in 2001, creating four constituencies for its people living abroad that would allow them to elect members to both houses of its Parliament. There are a few others, too, who allow this: Portugal and Tunisia, for instance. And needless to say, there is a growing demand coming now from other parts of the world. Some are mere whispers, while others are turning into gentle rumbles. This sort of clamour has typically been associated with right-wing parties since most expats tend to favour them. Basically, it is only when you are abroad that you rediscover your glorious heritage and glow with patriotic fervour—a sort of (to borrow the English writer T.H. Bailey's phrase) 'absence which makes the heart grow fonder'. Thus, in Italy, it was Silvio Berlusconi's idea to push for voting by expats and even creating constituencies for them. In France, this idea was pushed through literally in the last days of Nicolas Sarkozy's term. Not for nothing, was it viewed by many as a last-ditch effort to garner additional votes. Either way, both men did lose their jobs eventually.

Gerrymandering

Campaigning is not the only weapon in the armoury of the politician seeking re-election. An important arsenal constitutes redrawing constituency lines to one's advantage based on the knowledge of where voters live—an act referred to as gerrymandering. The term is named after Elbridge Gerry who, as the governor of Massachusetts, signed a bill in 1812 defining new senatorial districts. The story goes that the shape of the district that Governor Gerry drew was so bizarre that newspapers compared it to the mythical salamander (if you are interested you can find this image on the Internet), and named it 'Gerrymander' and the practice began to be called gerrymandering. In the US, all constituencies in a state must have roughly the same number of voters in it. So after every census, if it becomes clear that the population in an existing constituency (or district as they are referred to in the US) has changed, the boundaries may need to redrawn to ensure that there is an equal number of voters in every district.

This provides the party in power an opportunity to manipulate things through two different processes called 'packing' and 'cracking'. A packed district is drawn to include as many of the opposing party's voter base as possible. This helps the governing party to win in the surrounding districts where the Opposition's strength has been reduced by creating one packed district. So you lose one but gain many. Cracking does the opposite by splitting clusters of opposition voters among several districts, so that they are outnumbered in each district. Yes, it is the old divide and rule policy.

Some claim that the most blatant example of gerrymandering in India happened on 20 February 2014, when the Indian legislature passed the Andhra Pradesh Reorganisation Bill. This bill split the erstwhile state of Andhra Pradesh (with forty-two constituencies) into the two new states of Seemandhra and Telangana with twenty-five and seventeen constituencies, respectively. Afraid of losing to the BJP, it was believed that the Indian National Congress passed this bill to take credit for the creation of Telangana, and then by partnering with the Telangana Rashtra Samithi, the party would attempt to gain the seventeen constituencies. The US-style gerrymandering is difficult to achieve in India simply because an independent body called the Delimitation Commission of India is responsible for drawing the boundaries of constituencies. Independent India has had four of these commissions—in 1952, 1963, 1973 and 2002.[1] Interestingly, in 1976, delimitation was suspended till after the 2001 population census to ensure that family planning programmes being pursued by the different states would not affect their representation in the Parliament!

So, after about three decades, in 2008, political boundaries were redrawn in India. Economists Lakshmi Iyer and Maya Reddy took this opportunity to examine whether gerrymandering is an issue in India. Their findings are reassuring: using detailed demographic and electoral data, they found the redistricting process to be by and large politically neutral. The caveat: They found that there was no evidence of redistricting that would be unfavourable for politicians who were advisory members for the redistricting process. So, if any gerrymandering did take place, it is was rather limited and very local, making it an ineffective option.

Consequently, politicians in India, especially from the right, might want to go to the mountain and create overseas constituencies. I can easily see Prime Minister Narendra Modi getting a lot of votes from places like New Jersey which has a significant NRI (and Gujarati) population. But I can equally

---

[1]   Delimitation orders can be found at https://eci.gov.in/divisions-of-eci/delimitation/.

also see other parts of the world where the Shiromani Akali Dal or the Telugu Desam Party would do well. Keeping in mind that the Indian diaspora is significantly more heterogeneous than the population of the countries mentioned above—Philadelphia alone has a dozen or so churches for Malayali Christians serving different denominations—it may not be easy to predict the overall outcome. Although, based on what happened in the 2019 elections, Modiji will likely win. The other issue is that, unlike the citizens of all the countries mentioned above, given the inconveniences associated with immigration paperwork and travel, most Indians exchange their visas for citizenship within a few years of living abroad.

Practical Problems

In any case, I find the idea rife with practical difficulties. Imagine electing an MP for New Jersey, which, to some, is a vast suburb of New York City and to others the Garden State. To Indians, it is just a mini India. What will such an MP from this constituency, if it ever becomes one, accomplish, besides raking up a lot of frequent flyer miles? And who will pay for those frequent flyer miles? Most members of the constituency will already be paying their taxes to Uncle Sam. Surely, it's hard to justify undertaking such things using the Indian taxpayers' money. It is possible that the expat MP could push the issue of dual citizenship for Indians further, possibly do something about promoting Indian culture among their constituents deprived in this regard, raise funds for India, and also attract foreign direct investment. Although, I suspect most of the individuals who are in a position to contribute to this will already be American citizens. Of course, it will generate a feeling of warmth among the expats, who will now expect their voices to be heard, though I am not sure how to value that.

Whether this is a folly or a feasible option, only time will tell. At the moment, it remains an interesting notion that will probably gain popularity in a globalized world, where mobility keeps increasing and immigrant diasporas continue to grow. Who knows whether in the times to come winning in Louisiana and Belgium would matter as much as in Ludhiana and Belgaum in deciding a vote of confidence in the Lok Sabha!

Lessons from Stolen Shoes

A few years back, the *Telegraph* (UK) reported a story of cops in the Swedish city of Malmö nabbing a couple of gentlemen who were found stealing designer shoes from store windows. The funny thing was that only shoes meant for the left foot were on display in the shopfronts and therefore could be of no earthly use to anyone but one-legged people. Yet, this did not deter the thieves. Puzzled by this bizarre theft, the police dug deeper and uncovered a pan-Scandinavian gang of shoe stealers! It turned out that stores across the border in Denmark mostly exhibited shoes for the right foot in their display windows, whereas those in Sweden showcased only the ones for the left. Members of the syndicate whose operations the police uncovered were basically stealing left shoes from stores in Sweden and right shoes from stores in Denmark, to assemble designer pairs and sell in both countries.

I stumbled across the above parable of *chappalchori* or shoe pinching precisely while looking to highlight the idea of complementary goods: Left shoes and right shoes being the classic textbook example, I don't think I could have done better.

The Yin and the Yang

Complements play a significant role in our lives—bread without butter or jam, rum without coke, can all be problematic to varying degrees. Imagine *Chai pe Charcha* without chai. In some cases, we need a one-to-one match like one left shoe with one right shoe. Five left shoes with only one right shoe is the same as having one left and one right shoe. In other cases involving complements, the proportion may not be not fixed. You probably need more coke as the proportion of rum increases, but the amount of coke can vary from person to person. Complementarities are just as important in the production process—every programmer needs a computer, just as every call-centre person needs their phone and every farmer a ploughing or seedbed-preparation contraption.

This is an absurdly simple notion and one we are all familiar with. But it can have serious implications for economic development. A very stark example comes from an idea put forth by the 2019 Nobel Prize–winning economist Michael Kremer of Harvard University, labelled the 'O-ring Theory of Economic Development'. The notion here is that the skills of workers complement each other. The output in a factory, then, depends on all the skills being present and working together. In essence, the theory holds that even one weak link in the chain of production can have disastrous consequences—just as the single O-ring whose failure caused the 1986 *Challenger* space shuttle disaster. All that rocket science came to naught just because of the faulty design of a simple O-ring. An important implication of Kremer's theory is that if you take a worker from a less productive team and put them in a more productive team or country, their own marginal product (that is, how much additional output is created due to one's own effort), and therefore wages, will go up.[1]

---

[1]   This assumes, of course, that there are no horrible bosses and office machinations, and you get paid for what you add to the total output.

Coordination Failure

This notion of complementarity is important to keep in mind when creating teams or task forces, and also for understanding concepts such as brain drain, a phenomenon that occurs when workers from developing countries receive higher wages for the same skills by being deployed in more productive settings. Another crucial insight from the cross-country shoe thieves' story is the notion of coordination. If only the Danish and Swedish storeowners had coordinated to have all their stores uniformly display either left or right shoes, the chappalchori syndicate would have been out of business faster than you could say Salvatore Ferragamo.

Coordination issues are rampant in all spheres of economic activity—from choosing which side of the road to drive on to which software package to use when working with a group of people. A well-known theory of economic development is called the 'Big Push'. Postulated first by Paul Rosenstein-Rodan in 1943, it relies on the complementarities existing between different sectors of the economy. Sustained growth requires conscious attempts to invest simultaneously in all the sectors—hence the name Big Push. Often thought of as being similar to central planning, the theory fell into disregard till three smart economists—Kevin Murphy, Andre Shleifer and Robert Vishny—resurrected it in 1989, noting that the main issue was one of complementarities and coordination. Thus, the rail, steel and coal industries feed off each other (complementarities). If investment in either of these sectors lags behind (mis-coordination), it will pull the others sectors down and the economy may experience losses as the Swedish and Danish storeowners did. More importantly, failure to recognize the complementarity between them and investing in only one or two out of the three sectors can just lead to wasteful expenditure, like spending money on jam but not buying the necessary amount of bread to spread it on.

This is probably also most evident in another type of jam—traffic jams. Everyone living in a mid-sized or bigger city has to deal with them every single day. In fact, they only seem to get worse over time. I can still remember a time when very few people had cars, some had two-wheelers, but people mostly commuted on bicycles and public transport (where it existed). Roads were relatively empty. Then came the mopeds. They were not too bad—they did not crowd the roads, even though with their cavalier attitude they were mainly an irritant to all the others on the road. There were no traffic jams.

In the early 1990s, India liberalized and things were never the same again! Liberalization has brought about unprecedented growth, access to goods and services and, in general, a booming economy. Yet, it has not been without perils. One of the big changes that liberalization made possible was the development of the financial sector—in particular, the loan industry. It is now easy to get a home loan or an auto loan. However, no one paid heed to the fact that India did not have the roads to accommodate all these new vehicles that the easy-to-obtain loans would put on the roads. The private banking sector merrily went about its business of moneylending even though the complementary roads were not being built. As a consequence, today we (including those bankers) are all in a (traffic) jam![2]

---

[2]   Building more roads is not a solution to this problem. One option is to levy a very high tax on the purchase of any vehicle, akin to the luxury tax for eating at the Oberoi in Kolkata (the food there is really

Grey Markets

Back to chappalchori: In many parts of India, shoe theft enjoys legitimacy, if not pride of place, in weddings. It involves the bride's sister(s) hiding the footwear of the groom. The latter gets back his shoes, but only after protracted and often expensive bargaining with his sister(s)-in-law, causing much mirth and merriment among the onlookers. But a less glorious form of the shoe caper occurs in places of worship and occasionally on trains. Before entering temples, we are required to leave our shoes outside. There are many instances where on returning from a darshan, people find their precious footwear missing. The movie *Slumdog Millionaire*, in fact, picturized the young fake tour guides, Jamal and Salim, pinching shoes from outside the Taj Mahal and reselling them in the markets just a few kilometres from the monument. Apparently, Mumbai even has a well-known market in Kurla for trade in such stolen footwear.

A simple solution to the problem is, of course, is to wear ratty chappals. Alternatively, if you must strut your designer stuff, put them in separate cubbyholes.[3] People often express

---

good though, especially the breakfast). An alternative would be to do what the Chinese did in their big cities like Beijing. To be able to purchase a car, you need to win the car licence-plate lottery. The expected waiting time for winning is something absurd like fifty years. In the meantime, people were encouraged to use public transport, bicycles, mopeds or a taxi service. It is important to point out that taxis are relatively cheaper in China.

[3] This solution was first suggested to me by Professor Kaushik Basu. Some people argue that there is a negative correlation between the desire to wear designer stuff and being spiritual. Therefore, shoe theft strikes only those who deserve it!

shock at the audacity of those who pilfer shoes belonging to others, that too from places of worship. Heterogeneity among economic agents can easily explain this seemingly fearless act. Some people have more faith in the Almighty than others; those with lesser faith will gladly steal shoes and sell them. And the ones with still-lesser faith will also consciously buy such footwear if the price is right, braving the possibility of having to inherit the sins of those whose shoes they would now be slipping on.

In economic models, for instance, heterogeneity is a crucial factor that ensures trade can happen: If everyone was equally proficient in producing and wanted to consume exactly the same things, then what is the need for trade? The assumption of identical agents in economic modelling is intended primarily for finding solutions easily, thereby allowing us to gain the first level of insights with ease. Economists are cognizant of the fact that people are heterogeneous and subsequently allow for heterogeneity in their models. For instance, if I were studying how networks are formed among people, the baseline model would make an assumption that establishing a relationship in the network costs the same regardless of the identities of the persons involved. Similarly, the model would also assume that everyone provides identical benefits in the network. Only after having established what the stable/optimal networks would form under these simple conditions, would we try to introduce the notion that it may cost different amounts to link to different people. Similarly, different individuals might provide different levels of benefits. Heterogeneity among agents, thus, allows for a more realistic model and provides a sensitivity check; it tells us how good these (the initial easily found) solutions are in the real world, where people are not identical. Ultimately, it is heterogeneity that makes our models better and the world go around.

Résumés or Cereals—Packaging Matters

When the going gets tough, even the tough find it hard to land good jobs. And it's even harder for those not made of sterner stuff or people who simply cannot persevere with the job hunt. In a situation of economic slowdown with all the attendant uncertainty, finding employment requires that extra bit—of skills, luck, connections or a combination of these (ideally, all three). What further complicates matters is the fact that during a recession not only do employers cut back on hiring, thereby decreasing the supply of jobs, the demand for jobs also far exceeds the supply.[1] First, there are the usual new graduates seeking jobs. Then lay-offs induced by the recession add to the pool of job seekers. Therefore, any vacancy advertised during a recession is bound to receive an overwhelming number of responses. It is unclear how much effort overwhelmed prospective employers would undertake to examine each résumé, creating that niggling self-doubt: Will my résumé even get noticed?

One is usually told here to imagine an HR person sitting amidst piles of résumés and spending less than a minute to make a decision regarding whether or not to interview you. What matters, then, is that all the important information on your

---

[1] Observe that in the labour market the traditional roles are reversed—firms are the buyers of labour and individual consumers of firm output are the sellers of labour.

résumé hits a viewer—in this case, the HR manager—in the eye within thirty seconds. At least, that is what I tell my students!

The Right Résumé

Consequently, you need to choose the most appropriate résumé format to optimally showcase your skills and expertise for the industry and the job you have applied for. Thus, a one-page résumé may not be bad for an entry-level position in a corporate sector. On the other hand, for a job seeker in academia or those applying for senior positions in the corporate world, a curriculum vitae—or a 'long résumé' as it is sometimes called—may be more appropriate. In recent years however, many job seekers have abandoned the old, staid approach and have begun experimenting with their résumés to give them a distinct and vibrant look. For example, many applicants to the doctoral programme in my university nowadays put their pictures on their résumés. This has no connection to their GRE score, an important screening criterion, but perhaps the applicants feel that their application will stand out because now I can put a name and a face together. In their minds, they are no longer anonymous, faceless individuals for me.

We live in an age obsessed with using data and visuals to enhance how information is presented. This has led to résumé evolution: the 'infographic résumé' uses a visual timeline to present a person's skills. If you have not seen such a résumé and want to check one out, just log on to LinkedIn. You will find résumés using pie-charts, coloured tables and Facebook-style timelines aplenty. A testament to the popularity of such infographic résumés enjoy can be gauged from the profusion of websites offering free tools to create them.

Infographic résumés became fashionable from around 2002, especially in industries like marketing, graphic design and public relations. About five years later, the next stage of the résumé evolution began to take place. An alternative to the infographic résumé, called the 'video résumé', began to appear as yet another way to stand out in a pool of applicants. This one has the added advantage of providing the means to 'showcase' the applicant's communication skills and personality. I am sure other avatars in this evolution are already on the way . . .

Show You're Different

The infographic résumé is a classic example of 'product differentiation', a strategy used by firms to distinguish their products from that of rivals with an objective to appeal to specific groups of consumers. Since consumers tend to have different incomes and tastes, the same firm may actually create different versions of its product to appeal to these different market segments and, in turn, force its rivals to also create a bewildering range of products. Hence, Gillette sells several types of razors and Colgate-Palmolive provides a never-ending flow of slightly varied products to keep our teeth in order. And therefore, so do their rivals like Schick and Hindustan Lever.

The amusing aspect of product differentiation, of course, is how minimal such differentiation often is in reality. Not many may be able to differentiate between the taste of Pepsi and Coke; yet they will strongly prefer one over the other on being given a choice. Just walk into any supermarket in a big city to see product differentiation in full flow. Today, there are more than ten brands offering over seventy-five varieties of breakfast cereals, including cornflakes, oats and muesli. Twenty years ago, the only option the consumer had was, perhaps, Mohan Meakin's cornflakes. Ready-to-eat breakfast cereals are usually differentiated by their sugar content, crunchiness or the kind and quantity of fruits they contain.

The majority of Indians, however, prefer spices in every meal, including breakfast. So, unlike in most other countries, in India you will find that breakfast cereals range from sweet to several different types of savoury, spicy combinations like pepper and coriander oats. Our basic understanding of product differentiation stems from a seminal paper in 1929 by Harold Hotelling, a mathematical statistician who taught at Stanford, Columbia and the University of North Carolina.[2]

Imagine the main street of a small town along which all its consumers live. As a firm, where would you like to locate yourself on this street? For this, you would need to figure out what price to charge and how much consumers can afford to spend (in time and money) in getting to your store, and, of course, compare this with what your rival(s) have to offer in terms of their price and location on the main street. It is also reasonable to assume that a consumer will pick the store with the lowest

---

[2] Hotelling was a remarkable scholar who had a significant impact on statistics and economics. In statistics, he generalized the Student's t-distribution to the Hotelling's t-distribution and also developed the idea of principal component analysis. In economics, he is credited with establishing Hotelling's law, discussed here, and which, in many ways, laid the foundation for spatial economics and Hotelling's rule, which talks about how to think of pricing the extraction of non-renewable natural resources. He was also a fantastic mentor who is supposed to have influenced Nobel Prize–winning economists Milton Friedman and Kenneth Arrow. In addition, he is supposed to have helped bring statistician Abraham Wald over to the US to escape Nazi persecution.

effective price, that is, after considering the price of the product plus their travel time. Each firm uses this information, then, to choose where to locate itself in order to maximize profits.

Hotelling's paper posits this problem in terms of two ice-cream vendors choosing locations on a beach. The optimal choice for both, according to him, is to settle down in the middle and sell at identical prices. One vendor can cater to all the customers to the right of his cart, while the other one could serve all those to the left of his cart! And here we see Hotelling's brilliant insight: '[D]istance, as we have used it for illustration, is only a figurative term for a great congeries of qualities. Instead of sellers of an identical commodity separated geographically we might consider two competing cider merchants side by side, one selling a sweeter liquid than the other.'

In other words, having narrowed down their product to, say, masala oats, in the equilibrium identified above, the two rival firms will produce very similar products and charge similar prices! Which is to say that in equilibrium, we will observe what Hotelling called the '*principle of minimal differentiation*': masala oats, whether offered by firm A or firm B, will essentially taste the same.

Gulshan Kumar, the entrepreneurial genius who founded the T-Series music company, provided another very interesting example of product differentiation. While it is often alleged that the early fortunes of T-Series were from piracy, Gulshan Kumar's real success came from selling so-called cover versions of old Hindi movie hits. In these tapes, the music and the lyrics remained the same, but unknown singers (named in small print) provided their own rendition of the original songs. It allowed T-Series to launch low-cost and lower musical quality tapes at prices less than the original versions. In due course, Gulshan

Kumar also produced 'covers' of his own original singers, thereby effectively pirating himself!

True, the real Kishore Kumar or Mohammed Rafi lover knew the singers were different and wouldn't ever touch these tapes. But a majority of price-sensitive and not-so-discerning consumers simply didn't care. To give them the benefit of the doubt, their buying could also have had to do with a sheer love for variety—listening to different versions of the same song. A simple case of consumers seeking product differentiation for its own sake!

Postscript

If you are ready to take the plunge and differentiate yourself, visit http://vizualize.me/ and create your own infographic résumé. And for your next job search, especially when dealing with recruiters, try an experiment: Send the traditional résumé to some and the infographic one to others, and see for yourself what hits the eye more. Do not try this for a regular job application unless otherwise asked. Note that these are the author's personal opinions.

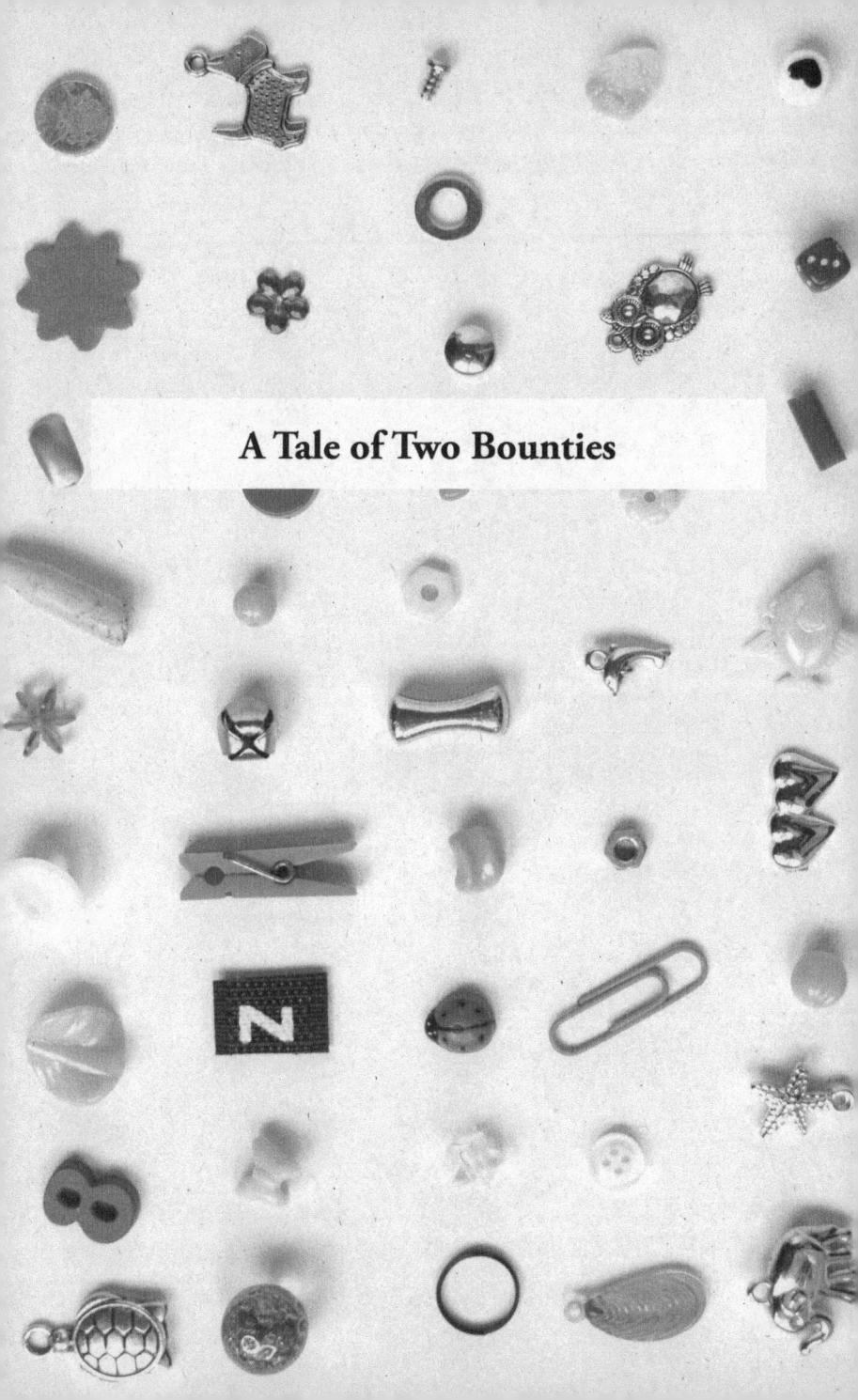

A Tale of Two Bounties

Bounties often produce strange outcomes. For instance, at the height of the Sudanese civil war in the nineties, a Zurich-based Christian group called Christian Solidarity International (CSI), moved by the plight of their brethren who were being enslaved by their Muslim victors, decided to intervene. After talking to several women and children who had been slaves and separated from their families, John Eibner, an official at CSI, decided to adapt an idea that was already in place to some extent. The local people often tried to negotiate or buy their kin out of slavery. Eibner decided to operationalize this idea on a large scale—very simply, he decided to buy freedom for large batches of slaves.

The Too-Big-to-Fail Argument

Imagine this: a rich white man from Switzerland shows up with a ton of money to give in exchange for the freedom of slaves. What happened as a consequence is quite predictable—numerous reports began to surface from Sudan about fake slaves (regular people pretending to be slaves) whose freedom was being exchanged for money. Some reports even suggested that offering a bounty for the slaves actually *encouraged* slavery, since it was now possible to make money by gathering up 'slaves' and setting them free in exchange for moolah. Note that in many cases, for such transactions, the actual religion of the slaves did not matter since they were fake slaves to start with! For instance, Santa would now agree to become Banta's slave so that they could both share the money from buying Santa's freedom. Moreover, they could do it repeatedly—possibly switching their roles as slave and slave owner. The point is that while incentives affect human behaviour in a positive manner, large incentives like bounties can also really distort behaviour.

This is the same reason that governments are reluctant to bail out banks, even those deemed 'too big to fail'. Once a bank realizes that the government will not let it fail, there is nothing to stop it from undertaking dangerous and risky activities. In fact, this is true for any borrower, large or small—there is no incentive for them to be careful with a loan, if they already know that they will eventually be bailed out. We will also have the same outcome if the borrowers know that their debt will be forgiven or they will escape criminal prosecution if they fail to repay the loan. The knowledge that their actions will not have adverse consequences does not encourage financial discipline.[1] Recall that the technical term for this is 'moral hazard' (formally, the lack of any incentives or desire to guard against a risk when you are protected from its consequences). The chapter on Muhammad Yunus's Grameen Bank explains how Grameen's group-lending strategy solves such a moral-hazard problem. Incidentally, this is also the reason why governments refuse to

---

[1] To a large extent, this is precisely the reason why several large borrowers were unable to pay and had to default on their loans in recent years. In other words, every Vijay Mallya or Nirav Modi that we fail to prosecute will only encourage other big borrowers to be financially irresponsible.

negotiate with terrorists and those who take hostages. Once you go down that path, you will encourage more hostage-taking!

Similar Instances in the Animal Kingdom

Interestingly, the actions of governments with regard to the culling of animals provides interesting instances of moral hazard. Apparently, worried about the number of cobras in Delhi, the British colonial government had started offering a bounty to anyone turning in a dead cobra. The story goes that in response to this, some smart people started farming cobras. As a result, the government finally had to kill the programme.[2]

The German economist, Horst Siebert, is supposed to have coined the term 'Cobra Effect' to describe this phenomenon in a book where he provides numerous examples of such perverse incentives—incentives that have unintended consequences and do not really solve the problem they are meant to solve. For example, in the nineteenth century, palaeontologists would travel to China and pay peasants for excavating dinosaur bones. Turns out that their compensation was based on the number of bones and not on their size. The Chinese peasants responded to this incentive in the most predictable way—when they found large dinosaur bones, they often broke them up into smaller pieces to maximize their compensation. While the story of the cobras in Delhi is largely anecdotal, apparently a similar thing did happen in Hanoi. The French colonial government in Vietnam offered a bounty on rats to rid the city of them,

---

[2] In fact, there is a *Freakonomics* podcast about this: http://freakonomics.com/podcast/the-cobra-effect-a-new-freakonomics-radio-podcast/.

with predictable consequences. This has been documented in an interesting study by historian Michael G. Vann.

Two Different Tunes

Now on to the tale of another bounty—one in which rodents still figured prominently, but it was a bounty that was never paid. In the year 1284, the German town of Hamelin was besieged by rats: these rats were a real menace. As the poet Robert Browning noted in his charming poem *The Pied Piper of Hamelin*:

> *They fought the dogs, and killed the cats,*
> *And bit the babies in the cradles,*
> *And ate the cheeses out of the vats,*
> *And licked the soup from the cook's own ladles . . .*

My favourite line appears a little later—the rodents even had the power to spoil gossip; as Browning puts it:

> *Made nests inside men's Sunday hats,*
> *And even spoiled the women's chats . . .*

The people of Hamelin were in despair and the Mayor was in the midst of an emergency meeting with all the movers and shakers in town, when a man dressed in colourful clothing (in all of the different accounts of this tale) walked in and offered to rid the town of its plague. Calling himself the Pied Piper, he claimed he had the magical power to attract all living creatures, and he especially used it against creatures harmful to man like the mole and the toad. He went on to state that his résumé (for that is what we would call it today) included ridding the ruler of Tartary of a swarm of gnats and the Nizam of Asia of vampyre bats! He offered that for 1000 guilders he would rid Hamelin of its rodent pestilence. The distressed Mayor gladly accepted his offer, and the Piper got down to business. As he played his pipe, rats came bounding out of every nook and cranny and they all followed him to their certain death in the river Weser.

The church bells rang out—Hamelin rejoiced!

The Piper went back to the Mayor and asked for his bounty. Unfortunately, the Mayor refused to pay up, saying that he was only joking about the money and instead offered the Piper 50 guilders. Here is how the Mayor actually put it to him:

> 'Beside,' quoth the Mayor, with a knowing wink,
> 'Our business was done at the river's brink;
> We saw with our eyes the vermin sink,
> And what's dead can't come to life, I think.'

Even though the Piper pleaded for his money, the Mayor did not budge. So finally, the angry Piper played a different tune, leading away almost all of Hamelin's children, leaving the adults repenting and grieving forever.

Strategically Speaking

This story has several interesting game-theoretic aspects. The Mayor, knowing that we humans do not have the power to bring back the dead, thought that he was playing the optimal strategy for this game by reneging on his offer. After all, what could the Piper do now? Given everything the Mayor knew at that point, his strategy was the best possible one, or what game theorists call 'subgame perfect', even if it was unfair. In layman's terms, an outcome is subgame perfect if a player is playing their optimal strategy, or the Nash equilibrium,[3] when it is their turn to move (or in every subgame of the game). Of course, this would have posed a different problem, if the Mayor was considering future interactions with the Piper or other people.[4] By refusing to pay, the Mayor was also destroying his reputation and that of the town of Hamelin forever. Nobody would want to conduct business with him or his town again.

To see this differently, imagine two countries—North and South. Now imagine that North makes a deal with South to build infrastructure, say, a railway track. Now, suppose the government in North that made this deal loses the election and the next government, for reasons of its own, reneges on the deal in the midst of construction. This is very bad for North's reputation and will have a significant negative impact on its ability to attract foreign direct investment in the future.

Is there a lesson in the story for the Piper? Certainly—if you have a secret weapon and you want to be paid for your work,

---

[3] John Nash formulated how to find the equilibrium of a simultaneous-move game (like Rock-Paper-Scissors), which is now eponymously called a Nash equilibrium.

[4] Situations where the same set of individuals interact with each other is called a repeated game. This is the subject of the chapter titled 'In God We Trust'. Building a reputation for being tough, or honest or even mean is not important if the parties don't plan to continue interacting in the future—such concerns are important only in a repeated-game context. Cola giants like Coke and Pepsi are aware that they will repeatedly compete with each other across time and space. Hence, building a reputation and a brand image is critical for them.

then it does not help to keep the weapon a secret. To provide a contemporary analogy, this would be the same as having the ability to make nuclear weapons, but choosing to keep the fact a secret. Many people today may not have watched this black-and-white movie simply because it was made in 1964—Stanley Kubrick's *Dr Strangelove*. In the movie, the Soviet Union claims to have a Doomsday Machine that cannot be dismantled or stopped if a nuclear attack is launched against them. Once activated, this Doomsday Machine will destroy the world. However, the American President's (former Nazi) adviser Dr Strangelove points out that this does not make any sense. Game-theoretically, such a machine is meaningful and can act as a deterrent only when *everyone* knows about it. Therefore, even though the Soviet ambassador says that the Soviet Union does have this machine, and they were planning to reveal its existence in the subsequent week, Dr Strangelove categorically dismisses this claim as a bluff.

Unfortunately, Dr Strangelove was wrong: the Soviets did have such a machine. After a sequence of crazy events, in the end there is nuclear annihilation and everyone (including the Soviets) loses. This is precisely the mistake the Piper also makes (or given the historical timeline, we should say the Soviets made the same mistake as the Piper)! The leaders of the town of Hamelin and in particular the Mayor did not know about his magical ability to enchant the children and follow his tune. Of course, it is possible that no one would have believed him without a demonstration of his flute's power over children, but he would have at least had a chance to get reimbursed. But then again, maybe the Piper never cared about his bounty, maybe he just did not want the children growing up in a town where the adults did not honour their promises.

Giving Credit Where Credit Is Due

Finally, I would like to point out that the original Pied Piper is Indian. When he touched his lips to the flute there was bungle in the jungle—the *gopi*s just could not stay away. Legend has it that regardless of the hour of the day, once the enchanted notes of Krishna's flute fell on their ears, they made whatever excuses they could—to their husbands or their parents—and rushed to the forest to frolic with Krishna. Now, this Piper, he did not need any game-theory lessons!

Why We Should Pay Our Domestic Help More

Finding domestic help is hard today. Even harder is retaining such help, assuming we are able to find them. It is next to impossible to find and retain good domestic help. One response to this problem has been the mushrooming of 'agencies' offering placement services of maids, cooks or drivers in exchange for a commission, often equivalent to at least two months' salary. These contracts, renewable every eleven to twelve months, are unstable, if not uneconomical, arrangements. Currently, the market for domestic workers is clearly a seller's market, i.e., the seller of labour or the worker themselves, now has more bargaining power than the buyer. This shift in the bargaining power in favour of the poorer participant (domestic worker) is a rather recent phenomenon. While I do feel sorry for ageing relatives who have to scramble from agency to agency, given the attrition rate among domestic help, I personally feel that this a welcome change. My goal in this piece therefore is to explain why it might be best for all if we pay our domestic help a higher wage.

A number of forces have contributed to the changing nature of the market for domestic workers. The first is liberalization and economic growth, both of which have brought about an expansion in job opportunities for skilled and unskilled workers. In particular, the construction boom has significantly contributed to this. Second, several welfare programmes initiated (by both well-meaning and populist politicians) in the last few years provide wage support—either directly through a programme like the Mahatma Gandhi Rural Employment Guarantee Act (MGNREGA), or indirectly in the form of highly subsidized foodgrains, midday meals to schoolchildren and other in-kind entitlement benefits. All these have increased the value of what we call the 'outside option', that is, the benefits that can be obtained by quitting the current job and going to the next-best or 'outside' option. Simply put, this means, given all the easy access to resources in cash or kind, it is no longer as attractive to seek employment as domestic help.

The growth of the construction sector has also created a demand for unskilled labour that could only work as domestic help earlier. Even though construction work in cities is demanding, it may be more attractive as an 'outside option', relative to what domestic workers have to contend with. They work long/odd hours, get no holidays or benefits and have very little freedom, while engaging in every conceivable task from cooking and babysitting to cleaning, washing and gardening. On top of all this, many of them may end up facing abuse and insults from their employers. Why bother with this type of work when a person can stay in the village and do MGNREGA work and some seasonal farm labour? In other words, alternative options that are attractive to the labour force are now available both in urban and rural India in addition to a variety of in-kind entitlements. The end result is that with so many alternative choices, the domestic-work sector has lost much of its appeal.

Consequently, while rising middle-class incomes in recent times have driven up the demand for domestic workers, their supply, driven by the changes in 'outside options', has gone down. It has led to an increase in wage rates in this market, but probably not enough. The 'shortage' of domestic workers we are seeing is, perhaps, only a consequence of their not being offered equilibrium market wages. This has a lot to do with middle-class attitudes that haven't kept up with the new growth realities and even their own rising incomes. Basically, wages at the lower end of the income distribution (including the domestic-worker sector) have simply not grown at the same rate as wages in the upper end of the income distribution. And this, I may add, is a global phenomenon contributing to rising income inequality everywhere along with all the other associated problems. Then, of course, true equilibrium wages must take into account things like the lack of holidays, odd work hours or psychological abuse that domestic workers have to suffer. Hence, my first suggestion for hiring domestic help is: *Offer true equilibrium wages.* Here is a simple tip for doing this: When negotiating with a potential domestic help, think of the alternatives available to this person, how demanding you are as an employer and also the rate at which your own income has grown.

Efficiency Wages

My second suggestion is that after having hired good domestic help, if we wish to retain them for long, we should consider going beyond equilibrium market wages. Pay higher than market wages—offer what economists call 'efficiency wages'. Henry Ford tried this first in 1914 and found that the company's productivity and profits went up significantly.

The efficiency wage theory suggests that if an employer pays higher than market wages, first it will ensure that workers don't shirk their duties. The reason being, they will be afraid of being fired from a job that pays more than what the market would pay. Second, since the incentive to shirk is reduced, it also means that you don't need to monitor your workers all the time. So you save on monitoring costs and have more peace, unless you are one of those control-freak micromanagers. Third, to the extent efficiency wages lead to lower turnover, the employer will also save on the cost of looking for a new worker, selecting one from among the applicants and the cost of training a new domestic worker every few months. Then there is the happiness factor—unlike Charlie Chaplin in *Modern Times*, research suggests that a happy worker (because they are getting a higher wage) will be more productive. The efficiency wages hypothesis argues that because the benefits are large enough, the cost of paying the higher wages is well worth it. Sociological models also relate this theory to notions of fairness. According to these, when workers believe they are being paid more than the market wages, they might feel morally obligated to reciprocate the kindness of their employer by working harder.

Besides, there are indirect benefits. For instance, an employer paying efficiency wages automatically minimizes the likelihood of being saddled with work shirkers. When you offer a higher than market wage, the applicant pool will be bigger and better, and you will have a higher chance of finding a better worker. Another question that is sometimes asked in the context of efficiency wages is the following: Since larger firms like an MNC will pay more than a smaller firm, does this have anything to do with efficiency wages? Yes, we can invoke efficiency wages to explain this wage gap. One could argue that larger firms have higher overhead costs and therefore incur higher expenditure when a worker quits. Therefore, they have strong incentives to offer higher pay to reduce turnover.

Finally, there are additional steps one can take beyond efficiency wages to hang on to great domestic help. You can borrow a leaf from the formal employment sector and offer your domestic help a certain number of holidays each month with the caveat that they have to inform you in advance. This will reduce those unplanned absences which leave you in the lurch and make for a happy employee.

Minimum vs Efficient

Workers who shirk responsibilities often tend to keep out of jobs paying higher than market wages since they are conscious of their own limited abilities. As already noted, the more diligent workers, however, are more likely to be attracted to the efficiency wage–paying jobs, signalling their better skills and ability. How do state-mandated minimum wages relate to efficiency wages? Note that a minimum wage is a like a floor—it sets the legal wage rate below which wages cannot fall. Minimum wages therefore clearly have to be above the market-equilibrium wage; otherwise, why would government intervention be needed at all? Setting the minimum wage below the equilibrium wage implied by the market demand and supply would just mean that the market would clear at the higher minimum wage. This would be yet another example of redundant legislation.

A minimum wage draws upon notions of morality and equity. Its implementation is seen as an attempt to improve the living standards of the poor, provide them dignity of labour and reduce poverty. To the extent of being above market-clearing wages, minimum wages would have all the benefits of efficiency wages. But the difference is that minimum wages have to be compulsorily paid in all sectors.

Efficiency wages, by contrast, are an effective strategy for sectors with high labour turnover rates. It is in the employers' own interest here to pay these wages without being prodded by the state.

One criticism of the efficiency wage theory is: What if all employers have the same bright idea and decide to pay efficiency wages? Won't this create excess supply of labour in the market, leading to unemployment? Well, the efficiency wages hypothesis does not necessarily imply an unemployment rate greater than the natural rate of unemployment.[1] Nor does it mean that workers who are unable to find a job in a sector that pays efficiency wages cannot work in some other sector at lower equilibrium wages!

In any case, however, it is highly unlikely that all of middle-class India will offer efficiency wages simultaneously, creating a glut in the market for domestic workers. In fact, given the remoteness of this possibility, the next time you are able to find a hard-working employee, go ahead and do something truly different: *Pay efficiency wages. See it as an opportunity, a win-win for both you and them!*

---

[1] The natural rate of unemployment is basically the idea that we cannot get zero unemployment, i.e., even when an economy is at 'full employment', there will still be some unemployment. This is attributed to a combination of frictional, structural and surplus unemployment. For instance, some people will be unemployed since they are between jobs, searching for something better.

Where the Mind Does Not Work

Talking on the cell phone while driving, eating while reading, or my personal favourite—chatting with the wife while continuing to work—are all examples of 'divided attention'. This term describes situations where we simultaneously, yet actively, pay attention to two tasks; I know some who can manage three or even four.

I first learnt about this concept while designing an experiment on 'recall'. Our team wanted to induce 'imperfect recall' among our subjects. Subjects in the experiments were shown road maps and expected to remember what they saw in a specific road map. One way, we thought to facilitate this experiment, was by dividing and conquering the brain's resources and having the subjects participating in our study do two different things simultaneously! So, while looking at road maps, the subjects would be shown a letter—A, B, C or D—briefly and later asked which letter they had been shown. Another common strategy was to ask the subjects to memorize a sequence of numbers or words while performing another task. Our *divide et impera* principle worked reasonably well. The attention of our subjects was split between the two tasks and we were able to show that more than half of our subjects could not recall what they had seen earlier in a perfect manner.

The Division of Attention

Divided attention, a notion put forth by psychologists, shows up in all spheres of life. Basically, it posits that we have a fixed amount of attention (like an attention budget) to split between different tasks. Therefore, simultaneously engaging in a second task affects a person's ability to recall information, perform any job with a lower error rate, identify patterns, distinguish between different types of sounds and, most certainly, one's ability to drive. Of course, divided attention may not be the only thing affecting one's ability to do a job well. Other things such as anxiety or intrinsic task difficulty can also impact one's performance in two simultaneous tasks.

But there is a silver lining for all those habitual multitaskers: We do have some scientific evidence showing that with practice you can do things better even with divided attention. George A. Miller, in a study in 1956, suggested that the working memory capacity of human beings (roughly to be understood as our ability to juggle facts and perform mental operations) is limited to seven units. It means that if you are shown simple images—a geometrical object, a string of numbers or musical notes—and asked to recall how many of these things you encountered, you will do fine so long as there are seven or less of these objects. But, in general, when you have to deal with multiple tasks at the same time, a cognitive constraint kicks in and affects your performance in these tasks.

Toll on Cognition

The poor are often blamed for not being focused, which seemingly leads them to making bad decisions. There are many who even consider it as an intrinsic character trait: If they worked harder, they could better their lot! However, a study published in the prestigious journal *Science* has argued that poverty by itself imposes a heavy tax on one's cognitive abilities. We cannot blame the poor for their lot, because their immediate financial worries leave them with much less mental bandwidth to deal with other problems relative to those who are better off. That, in return, gets reflected in their cognitive capacity and makes them prone to errors.

The authors of the study (Anandi Mani, et al.) have estimated that being poor is equivalent to having about 13 IQ points less, or being a chronic alcoholic, or losing an entire night's sleep![1] How? Well, dealing with uncertain incomes and juggling finances to make ends meet is a difficult task, and the result is divided attention, which imposes a cognitive load, making it harder to concentrate and grapple with other issues in a successful manner. Among other things, this may explain why poor people fail to stick to drug regimens, are less productive workers, may make poor choices as parents and make worse financial decisions.

IQ and Poverty

In order to establish this, the authors carried out two experiments—one with shoppers in New Jersey and the other with sugar-cane farmers in Tamil Nadu. Four hundred shoppers in a New Jersey mall were randomly assigned to either a 'hard' or an 'easy' *hypothetical* financial task. The easy task required the participants to ponder over a scenario where

---

[1] Keep that in mind when you pull your next all-nighter studying for an exam or to complete that project you have to present.

their car repair would cost $150, while the difficult task asked them to consider a situation where the car repair would cost $1500. The subjects had an annual median income of $70,000, while the lowest income was around $20,000. The median income was used to split the sample into two groups—those with incomes of $70,000 or more were considered rich while the others were considered poor. Once their brains were cued in to thinking about their assigned tasks, they were asked to solve standard IQ-type problems. It turned out there wasn't any significant difference between the rich and the poor when they were assigned the easy task. But the poor participants performed significantly worse than the rich when assigned the hard task. Recall the participants were asked to *imagine* that their car needed a cheap or expensive repair—it is not like their car actually needed a repair. As Jiaying Zhao, one of the authors of this study, put it, 'Just asking a person to think about hypothetical financial problems reduces mental bandwidth. This is an acute, immediate impact, and has implications for scarcity of resources of any kind.'

In Tamil Nadu, the researchers recruited 454 sugarcane growers from the Villupuram and Tiruvannamalai districts. The study compared their relative performance in tasks similar to the ones already described at two different points in time—when the same farmers were poor (one month before the harvest) and rich (one month after the harvest). The effect, in terms of IQ points, was somewhat lower for the farmers (about 9–10 IQ points as opposed to 13 IQ points), but it was still distinctly present and was a robust finding even after controlling for a number of potential confounds like quality of nutrition, available time, stress levels and the fact that the farmers may get better at the IQ tests by doing them a second time.

As Anandi Mani put it, 'We're finding that when he has more money, he [the farmer] is more intelligent, as defined by IQ tests.' There are two observations I would like to make at this point. First, the shoppers in New Jersey definitely would not qualify as destitute. And incidentally, since it was New Jersey, many of those shoppers might have been of Indian origin. Second, the farmers in Tamil Nadu may have exhibited a smaller effect, but they are not individuals living in abject poverty. Now imagine how round-the-year poverty can affect the truly poor!

It should not be hard to see that poverty then begets poverty. Impaired cognitive function brought about by poverty can lead to more errors and poorer decisions which further their poverty. For example, they might have to borrow money from a payday loan shop or from the extortive village moneylender.[2] Essentially, as another author of this study, Sendhil Mullainathan, explained, it is not just the poor, but anyone experiencing destitution cannot ignore their circumstances and the subsequent consequences.

Designing Policy

The study clearly suggests some new ways to deal with poverty—given their cognitive overload, it is important to simplify things for the poor. Typically anti-poverty programmes focus on the

---

[2] The chapter titled 'One for All and All for One' studies the activities of the village moneylender or sahukar in more detail. A payday loan operation in the US is a place where if you have a stable job, you can borrow money against your future pay cheque. The lender simply takes your pay cheque when it arrives. Naturally, the interest rates are exorbitant.

fact that the poor lack material resources and ignore the fact that they also lack mental resources. So one important policy takeaway from this study is that we need to cut down on red tape. As the fourth co-author of this study, Eldar Shafir, puts it, 'You want to design a context that is more scarcity proof.' Every government programme aimed at the poor needs to have simple forms and perhaps proper instructions for filling them out. Things like pushing poor families in the right direction or providing them reminders might be equally important here. Thus, simplifying the process of interaction between the government and the poor might be no less important for the war against poverty. Maybe, this is too much to ask for in a country where to receive your pension, you have to typically prove that you are alive by physical presence.[3]

In any case, Professor Anandi Mani and her team have provided us an important insight regarding scarcity and mental capacity. Something to keep in mind in this age of multitasking where we are constantly expected to process more (readily available) information and deliver better results![4]

---

[3] I know this for a fact because my father typically has to do this at least once every year.
[4] Here is a simple test to check if your attention was divided while reading this essay: How many authors did this study have? Bonus question: What were their names?

Pens in Pockets

Many readers may not remember those times—some of you were probably not even born—when the pen was not just mightier than the sword, but it was also *a symbol of status*! Indeed, pens were a ubiquitous presence in pockets. I remember everyone—well, maybe not everyone, but most people—carrying at least one. And these were mostly fountain pens. The coveted brands were Sheaffer, Parker, Cross and Waterman. Even back then, the less affluent resorted to Chinese makes which, not surprisingly, were also a favourite among college students: I personally remember using the likes of Wing Sung, Doctor and Hero pens.

But those days are gone.[1] Today is definitely another day, actually a different era. We rarely see people carrying pens, let alone showing them off. And if they do, it's usually plain ballpoint pens whose *differentia specifica* seems to be their innate tendency to get lost or go missing just when they are needed, causing varying degrees of irritation to their owners.

So What's Changed?

One argument for fewer pens in pockets today is that technology has rendered them somewhat obsolete. It is akin to

---

[1] A fascinating history of fountains pens in India can be found in Bibek Debroy's recent monograph, *A Fountain Pen Story*.

the phenomenon of fewer people wearing watches these days because they have things like Fitbits and smartphones. The plethora of smart devices and their vast range of functionalities has probably made carrying a pen redundant.

But I contend there's more to this story. Let me explain why. Recently, I met a friend from IIT Bombay at a conference organized by the department of mathematics at Dibrugarh University, Assam. I was surprised to see him still carrying a fountain pen in his pocket. When I expressed my surprise, he told me the following story.

Once, as a little boy, this friend of mine happened to go to the post office in his village in Andhra Pradesh. Just before putting his letter in the mailbox, he realized he had not written the pin code. When he asked the man at the post office for a pen, the latter shot back: 'Don't you go to school? What kind of educated person are you if you do not even have a pen?' Since that day, some thirty years ago, my friend claims to have never stepped out of the house without a pen in his pocket! The point I am trying to make is that there was a time when education was highly prized in India. It still is, but back then it was a scarcer commodity. There weren't as many engineers and doctors around. Overall literacy rates, too, were lower. Besides, the number of job options in pre-liberalized India were limited, making an education all the more desirable. So, the ones who had it, flaunted it. And one certain way to do so was to display a pen in the pocket!

This was what economists would call the classic signalling model at work. The basis for it lies in asymmetric information. To explain: In many economic transactions, the parties involved do not possess the same information, whether of a quantitative or a qualitative nature. For example, a doctor typically has more information about diseases than a patient. A bank is less likely to know about a borrower's creditworthiness, which makes it harder to lend to those who have no collateral or a credit rating (the reader may refer to the chapter on Grameen Bank for more on this topic). Similarly, a buyer of a flat under construction is less likely to know if it will be delivered on time than the project's promoter. Two things are certain though: First, we can safely assume that the flat will never be delivered on the original date the builder of the flat promises. Second, builders who have developed more than one set of properties acquire a reputation for their timeliness and this allows flat buyers to predict the extent of the delay (incidentally, the role of reputation and why rational individuals may not wear seat belts is discussed in the chapter titled 'In God We Trust').

But let's focus on a situation more relevant to our purpose. Consider a firm seeking to hire new employees. In this case, the prospective employee is likely to be more aware of his or her abilities than the potential employer. Whether it is for a high-skill or low-skill job, the employer simply cannot tell by looking at an employee or their résumé whether they will be a good or a bad worker.[2] The employee, on the other hand, knows how good or bad they are. This, then, creates information asymmetry, which the market mechanism cannot ordinarily resolve. The problem for the employer is that both the good and bad workers will pretend they are good workers—everyone knows that the employer will only want to hire the most productive workers.

---

[2] The résumé, however, does reveal some information about the potential employee, like what type of education a person has and where they got it. This, as we will see, is useful.

Signalling Economics

It was Michael Spence, winner of the Nobel Prize for economics in 2001, who first proposed the notion of signalling. Spence has been associated with Harvard, Stanford and, more recently, New York University and Bocconi University in Milan, Italy. His PhD advisers were Kenneth Arrow (Nobel Prize, 1972) and Thomas Schelling (Nobel Prize, 2005). It is probably not a surprise that those who know him consider his mind to be a racing car! His most famous students are Bill Gates and Steve Ballmer who have both claimed that they mostly skipped class.

Consider a market with asymmetric information. The abstract idea behind signalling is that those with a higher ability may improve the market outcome by taking costly action to signal information to poorly informed recipients. In a classic 1973 paper, Michael Spence showed how education could act as an effective signalling device in the job market prone to information asymmetry. *By acquiring more education, even if not relevant to the job at hand* (and this is a key part of the insight), a prospective employee could suggest to the employer that they are a person of higher ability.

Education, in fact, satisfies all the characteristics of a good signal. First, it comes at a cost. In terms of money, time and effort, only those with the appropriate ability will invest in acquiring higher education. For instance, I would not invest in learning music even if someone paid me to do it. It would be a waste of my time and their money. Second, it is verifiable since one can furnish a degree to prove it. This is one reason why firms look at your résumé to assess how much education you have. They also check from where you have got your degrees. Thus, having an IIT or an IIM degree signals higher ability than a non-IIT or non-IIM degree. Note that it does not say that a person from another institution cannot have higher ability, it is just that their degree does not *signal* the same level of ability as one from these elite institutions. They have to resort to other means—say, for example, their first job was in a highly reputed firm or their first publication was in a highly reputed journal.

Interestingly, economists have documented that people tend to seek more education during economic downturns. When jobs are hard to find, the opportunity cost of education is lower. So you educate yourself more and wait for the economy to recover. But at this point there will be a large number of job seekers; a greater level of education ends up giving you the edge for competing with this pool of workers since it allows you to signal your higher abilities. Similarly, in pre-liberalization India (before the emergence of private-sector driven higher education), when education opportunities were fewer and education itself was scarcer, it had a more significant bearing in finding jobs and declaring one's status. Thus, carrying a pen in the pocket was a signalling device that confirmed membership in the educated class.

Of course, this raises a question: What stopped the less educated from mimicking the more educated by keeping pens in their pockets? The answer is simple—you can fool people some of the time but not all the time! While carrying a pen in the pocket may not be a costly signal, the person's credentials could still be easily verified, for instance, just by talking to them. In my grandfather's village, there was a man whose son worked in Bombay and had bought his father a fancy-looking fountain pen, which the gentleman proudly displayed in his pocket. However, if you asked him to write a letter or an address for you—as was common in villages in those days of no texts and emails—he would always find an excuse for not doing it. Everyone knew why, and I can recall several instances when people would just ask the said gentlemen to write something just to hear his latest excuse! Incidentally, signalling is rife in the animal kingdom. Take peacocks for instance, a brighter plumage signals that they will be better mates. By contrast, nature has made the peahen rather dowdy-looking, and assigned the task of fighting for mates to the peacocks.

The Alternative: Screening

Signalling is only one way to solve the asymmetric-information problem. While potential employees may resort to it, employers also have other means to make their selection. That includes everything from time spent sifting through résumé to interviews and exams which form a part of the selection process to sort out the wheat from the chaff. Economists call this 'screening', and the movie industry which screens films calls it auditioning.

But screening is costly and the costs are borne by the employer. This is why referrals are very important for getting jobs. Your friend knows you well. So when they refer you to an employer, the employer has to choose between a worker whose quality is known (you) versus finding one from the pool of applicants through the costly process of screening. The choice is obvious. On the other hand, signalling imposes costs on the potential employees. In practice, the labour market looks for a reasonable mix of the two—signalling and screening.

Now, back to why pens in pockets are no longer ubiquitous. First, India today is a more literate country and therefore it is possible that the pen signal is not as meaningful. But most likely it is because the post-liberalization Indian economy values not just Saraswati (education) but also Lakshmi (money). Hence, the signalling devices have changed. We flaunt our smartphones—this is a sign both of our education and our wealth! What does this mean for the humble pen? Since it has ceased to be a signalling tool, the pen has been reduced to its basic functionality—a simple writing instrument. A sharp contrast to what Bibek Debroy in his book on fountain pens says, 'Portraits, pictures and statues of Babasaheb Ambedkar often show him with a fountain pen in his hand or pocket, a symbol of modernity; Gandhiji, meanwhile, is depicted with his reed pen. One might say that the exchange of the reed pen for the fountain pen is illustrative of India's economic transition.'

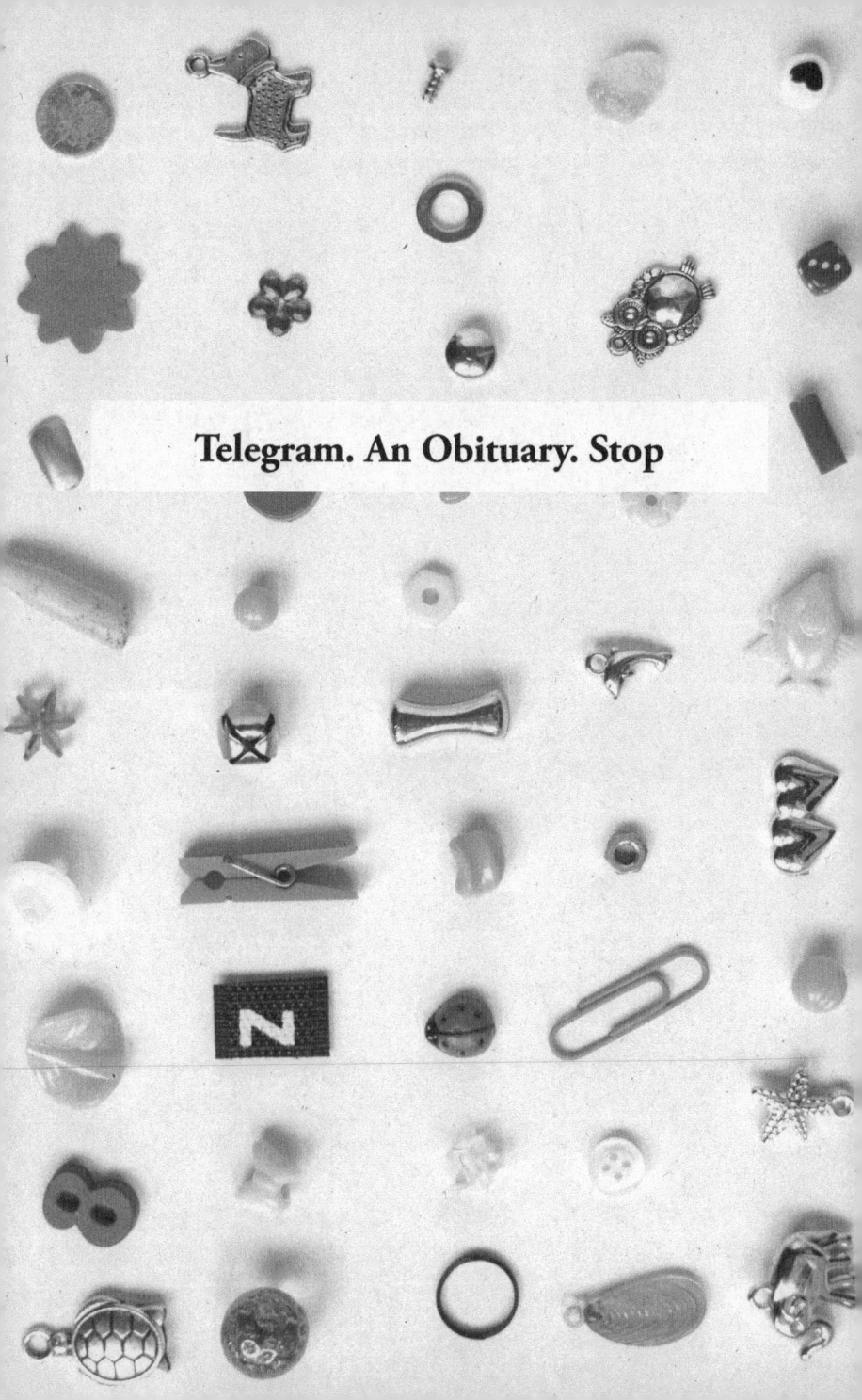

Telegram. An Obituary. Stop

Recently, while discussing a problem involving communication and precision of signals in economics over lunch, somehow, the fact that we would no longer be able to send telegrams in India cropped up.[1] One of us representing the younger generation (my former doctoral student—Chandan Jha) confessed, somewhat embarrassedly though, that he had no clue what a telegram was, even though he had heard of the term. No wonder then, concluded the other shocked author with the greying beard (that is me), the only ones who really protested the termination of Bharat Sanchar Nigam Ltd's (BSNL) telegram services were the state-owned company's employees who stood to lose their jobs!

I then proceeded to recount my favourite telegram story: Back in the day, when I was a student in Delhi, the hostel I was staying in had just one phone for its 100-plus residents. This solitary instrument was unavailable most of the time to most of the residents, since it was hogged by the half-a-dozen Romeos who clung to it to make up for the physical absence of their Juliets. Hostellers those days typically communicated with their

---

[1] 'Recently', you see, is a relative term. The said lunch took place in Baton Rouge, Louisiana, sometime in July 2013.

parents by means of letters and were always on the lookout for that most important of all missives—the money order.

Cut to the Present

One day, the erstwhile (young) author received a telegram from his folks, who hadn't heard from him for some time. It just said, 'Silence causes worry.' Not to be outdone, he immediately rushed to the post office and fired back: 'Speech is silver, silence golden.' That was enough for his parents to breathe a sigh of relief. Despite the lack of missives or vocal communication from their dear son, silence wasn't cause for worry any more. Those five telegram words were confirmation that he was fine. As my conversation with Chandan ambled along, it became clear to us that the three most important aspects of communication are speed, precision and relevance. Incidentally, there is an app these days that goes by the name Telegram which is a messaging service that claims to have all these qualities and security as well.

In this age of email and texts, we can receive and send messages quicker, at much lower costs and with greater efficiency. Telegrams, on the other hand, were relatively slow and expensive. They also needed to be very precise and used only when required—not necessarily always as a harbinger of bad news. For instance, in 1985, there were 45,000-odd post offices across India that sent and received some 60 million telegrams—*taar*, literally, wire, in local language—a year. That number had since fallen to an estimated 1.8 million by 2013, with only seventy-five offices remaining in operation. And with effect from the night of 15 July 2013, BSNL has ceased to offer this service altogether.

While receiving a telegram could (we can now, indeed, talk in the past tense) take up to two days, one can send and receive messages via cell phones and the Internet almost instantly. Moreover, the latter options can be used for both verbal and visual communication. While a telegram of up to fifty words would have cost the sender roughly Rs 27, it is practically costless to send a text message (which is typically shorter), with the added benefit of instant delivery. It is even better with emails, where messages of practically any length can be instantly sent for free! But it wasn't at all like this when cell phones first became operational in India and VSNL started its Internet services around 1995. It took another ten years for these to be available at affordable costs to the *aam aadmi*, the common man. Thus, for around 150 years—the Indian Post and Telegraph Act of 1854 is proof of it—the telegram remained the most cost-effective and, hence, most used means of speedy communication.

Fixed Cost Economics

There is one major cost aspect distinguishing the current modern means of communication from the antiquated telegraph: fixed costs. To send a text message or an email, you need a cell phone or a computer and also pay a monthly service fee. In other words, there is a fixed cost for accessing the technology, though once that is paid, the marginal cost of an email or text message is virtually zero. That is, once you set up your computer or mobile, each additional message costs zero. As more and more messages are sent, the cost per message or average cost (variable cost plus fixed cost) also approaches zero. This is a typical feature of all information goods: they have high fixed costs with zero marginal costs. This holds true for buyers and sellers, though not necessarily for the same product. For example, it is costly to create software (high fixed costs), but to put it on CDs or distribute over the Internet is practically costless for the software developer. Similarly, once you have a Netflix subscription, you do not have to pay for each additional movie you watch.

In the case of a telegram, the user does not incur a fixed cost, but there is a substantial marginal cost for every taar that is sent. As a result, telegrams were used mainly in exceptional circumstances—like what was once encountered by the shocked author with the greying beard in his younger days.

The Downside

The zero marginal cost of sending emails and text messages naturally engender a tendency for overuse. Hence, one tends to receive unwanted stuff, meaning, we now have to set aside time for separating the important messages from the trivial. We all probably know that one person who keeps filling our mailbox with silly jokes that they wouldn't have forwarded using a telegram. We have all got text messages or telemarketing calls at inopportune moments, besides hearing stories about senior citizens defrauded through some email-mediated financial scam.

The fact that 'spam' usually does not come with an opt-out provision for the receiver can, by itself, impose significant costs. According to the 2013 Internet Security Threat Report, despite a substantial decline in percentage terms, about 30 billion spam messages were sent daily to valid email addresses in 2012. I have no idea what the number looks like these days with everyone using applications like WhatsApp and WeChat. Spam generates what economists call 'negative externalities'. An externality is a cost or benefit for some other person(s) that a consumer or producer does not take into account. When you choose to get vaccinated, or wear a face mask in the time of Covid-19, for instance, not only do you protect yourself from the disease, you can now no longer pass it on to others. Hence, you lower the probability of other people contracting the disease as well. Thus, vaccinations generate positive externalities by reducing everyone's probability of getting the disease, whereas something like smoking creates negative externalities by imposing costs on passive smokers too. Typically, the person making the decision to get vaccinated or smoke does not take this externality into account when making their own choices. Spam imposes negative externalities since senders simply don't care about the burden they impose on the hapless lot of receivers. Economists Justin M. Rao of Microsoft Research and David H. Reiley of Google Inc. found that while the benefit to spammers from their activities worldwide was worth only $200 million a year, the cost to American firms and consumers alone was $20 billion at the most conservative estimate.

Let me tell you about another externality that is being caused by cheap and easy communication, and it is one we should all care about. If applying for a job simply requires pressing a button instead of having to send a job application by post as in the old days, then one may see job seekers applying for any and every job they come across, even when they know that the job is not a good fit and that they only have a remote chance of getting it. After all, a drowning man will clutch at straws. Imagine every job seeker doing this. Now, the potential employer has to spend time, money and effort screening through a stack of applications, of which a significant number actually constitute spam. Apart from the effort involved in screening, it probably also reduces the efficiency of the employer's search process resulting in bad matches, i.e., both the employer and the employee lose out!

Dare I say then that given the lack of fixed costs and zero costs of dealing with spam, the end of telegrams may spell bad news beyond its effects on BSNL employees. The good news, however, is that International Telegram launched its telegram services in India in the month of July 2013. Ironically though, you'll need an Internet connection to send a telegram online through its itelegram. com website. Interestingly, the first rapid long-distance telegraph communication system known as 'semaphore' used smoke signals, beacons and reflected lights. A bunch of enthusiasts in France have been trying to relocate the old semaphore message stations that preceded the advent of the electric telegraph to understand how they were used so efficiently by Napoleon, who created them for quick military communication.

Those who fear that they will miss their telegrams or never get one should not despair. Who knows, quite possibly in the near future, some neo-Luddite enthusiasts might revive this seemingly antiquated communication tool.

Until then . . . AU REVOIR STOP.

Rereading an Old Gandhi Essay

In recent years, historians, both revisionist and radical, have heaped criticism on the Father of the Nation; it used to be and is still fashionable to do so. Indeed, Gandhi himself provided the material that has added grist to the mill—when it came to food and sleep he did have some odd habits. But in my mind, he was first an astute political leader who gave to the world a unique form of protest, the non-violent mass protest, that ultimately was largely responsible for the British quitting India. Whatever his personal quirks, one cannot deny him this contribution! Moreover, there are no political leaders, perhaps anywhere in the world today, capable of doing (and willing to do) what he did nearly a century ago.

For about a year, after returning to India from South Africa in 1914, Gandhi traversed the length and breadth of India by train, in third-class compartments—which incidentally no longer exist[1]—just to learn about the common man and his country. Can we name a single leader today who would try to 'learn' about the aam aadmi—whom they are supposed to be serving—in such a direct manner? And not to mention our politicians who have tried to oppose the law that bars candidates with criminal backgrounds from holding elected positions.

---

[1] I can just imagine today's netas saying—how can I emulate him when third class no longer exists in Indian trains?

Like the intrepid Gujarati that he was, Gandhiji went to South Africa in 1893 to work as a lawyer after earning a barrister's degree in London, but failing to build a practice in India even after trying for two years.[2] It was South Africa, a country rife with racial discrimination, which actually transformed Gandhi from an ordinary struggling professional to the Mahatma that he later went on to become. One particular experience had a strong impact on the otherwise quiet and shy Gandhiji—the 'Pietermaritzburg incident', as it is sometimes referred to, when he was thrown out of a first-class train compartment. Not because he did not have a valid ticket but because of the colour of his skin. Pietermaritzburg happened during Gandhi's very first year in South Africa. It was probably not a coincidence, therefore, that on returning to India, he first decided to 'learn' about his country and its people by travelling in trains—this time, only by third class.

In 1917, he also penned an essay titled 'Third Class in Indian Railways'.

Train of Thoughts

Although there are visible signs of change, a lot of what Gandhiji said in his essay about the filth and squalor in Indian trains and railway platforms resonates even today. Reading it also makes you realize that while the Indian Railways has improved

---

[2] Incidentally, I call Gujaratis the explorers of India—they will happily go where no Indian has ever gone before. For example, in the early 2000s, I had gone to Machu Picchu and found only one Indian restaurant in Lima, Peru. The owner was Gujarati and the food was excellent.

considerably, the fact that we no longer have a third class has actually only been of cosmetic significance at times.

However, there is one issue raised in the essay on which I would disagree with Bapu—and I'm sure he wouldn't have taken offence. It has to do with the comparison he makes of the travel conditions of first-class passengers with those travelling by third class. While noting how first-class fares are five times that of third-class travel, Bapu goes on to ask: 'Does the third-class passenger get one-fifth, even one-tenth, of the comforts of his first-class fellow? It is but simple justice to claim that some relative proportion be observed between the cost and comfort.'

Justice—or the lack of it—in the realm of pricing goods and services was what Bapu was alluding to here. Unfortunately, the logic of economics works differently. I am not saying this is right or wrong; it is just that in matters of pricing, there may be simple economic motives at work making things seem unjust. The reason why 'simple justice' and a simple link between 'cost and comfort' does not work in pricing is because people have different tastes. Hence, they are prepared to pay different prices for the same product.

Logic of Pricing

A diehard Shah Rukh Khan fan may not mind paying more for his movie than what someone swearing by Salman Khan would. So, we have two people willing to pay different prices to watch the same movie in the same seat of the same theatre for the same show! A seller would ideally want to charge every buyer the maximum amount they are willing to pay for the product. But buyers do not walk into a store and tell the seller the maximum amount they are ready to pay. One way through which firms try to get around this problem is by engaging in a practice called 'price discrimination'.

This involves the same seller selling identical goods at different prices. Examples of this phenomenon are a dime a dozen. For instance, when you buy something in bulk, the seller gives a quantity discount. Since students often have less money, they get price discounts in many cases, on producing a valid student ID. Another interesting example one can quote is the entry fee for the Taj Mahal, with Indians having to pay Rs 50 while foreigners must shell out Rs 1300—a difference of 2500 per cent. Also, I am told that the guards at the Taj entrance are very savvy—they can tell by just looking whether you are Indian or not! Some friends of mine of Indian origin who recently visited the Taj were told by the entrance guards that while they could pass off as locals, the Yankee accent of their kids made it unnecessary to even examine their passports. So my friends had to pay the Rs 1300 rate for their two children.

Another way to engage in price discrimination is by letting buyers self-select. Thus, when firms put out coupons, price-sensitive consumers will clip and use them, while other buyers will not take these pains. Similarly, airlines offer more expensive business class seats with greater luxuries and also cheaper no-frills economy seats. Note that price discrimination will not work if you can't prevent resale. If I could buy a product in bulk or with a student ID and sell it to others at a higher price, the original seller stands to lose out. Just as resale will prevent successful price discrimination, business class travellers need to be prevented from buying economy tickets. Clearly, if the economy seats offered sufficient luxury (the relative proportion between economy fare cost and extent of comfort), those otherwise willing to pay business class fares would switch to economy class travel.

Discrimination Justified?

Jules Dupuit, a French civil engineer, explained this really well in the context of train travel. I will just reproduce what he said:

> It is not because of the few thousand francs which would have to be spent to put a roof over the third-class carriages or to upholster the third-class seats that some company or the other has open carriages with wooden benches. What the company is trying to do is to prevent the passengers who can pay the second-class fare from travelling third-class; it hits the poor, not because it wants to hurt them, but to frighten the rich. And it is again for the same reason that the companies, having proved almost cruel to the third-class passengers and mean to the second-class ones, become lavish in dealing with first-class passengers. Having refused the poor what is necessary, they give the rich what is superfluous.

Dupuit wrote this in 1849, twenty years before Gandhiji was born. It is unlikely that Bapu would have read Dupuit. Either way, he wouldn't have agreed, for he couldn't stand discrimination of any type. As the punchline of the film *Lage Raho Munna Bhai* goes, '*Bande mein tha dam, Vande Mataram*'! This man, indeed, had the guts to be different.

It might be of interest to the reader that this essay was first written on the occasion of the 144th birth anniversary of Mohandas Karamchand Gandhi, whom we affectionately call Bapu, or Father of the Nation.

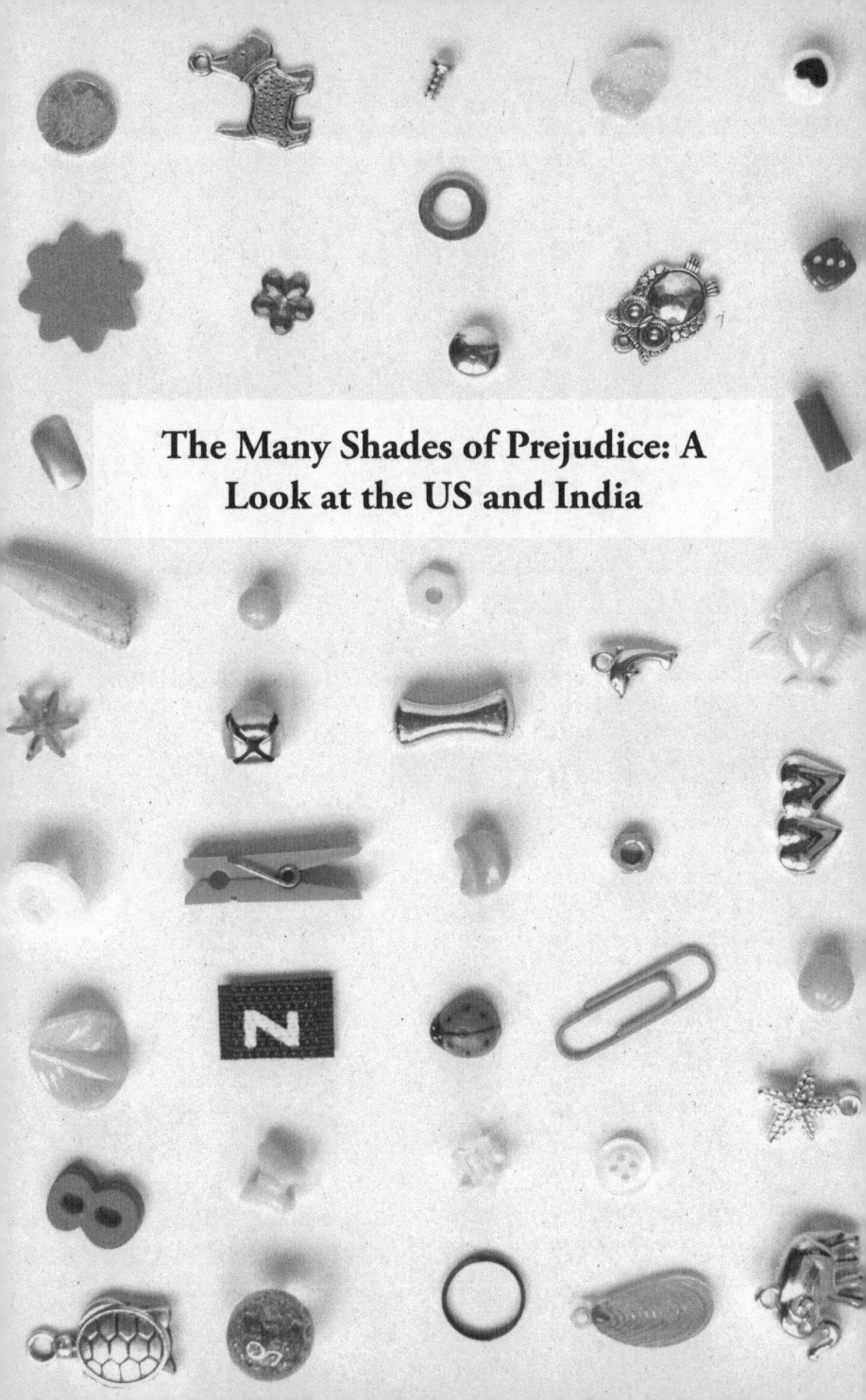

The Many Shades of Prejudice: A Look at the US and India

This is an issue that I first wrote about in 2015, but it is even more prescient today. We live in a world that is becoming increasingly polarized and we frequently hear about conflicts between groups within the same country. I am referring to the rise of white supremacists in the US and the lynching of Muslims in India—I do not recall such events growing up. I grew up listening to *Ek Chideeya, Anek Chideeya* songs on Doordarshan in an era when the key mantra in India was 'Unity in Diversity'!

I first wrote about this topic after watching a video showing a South Carolina policeman shooting down an unarmed man as he was running away in April 2015; needless to say, it created a furore all over the US. It reminded people of a similar incident that had occurred the previous August in which an eighteen-year-old boy, again unarmed, was shot dead by a police officer in Ferguson, Missouri. A number of other such incidents have occurred—the killing of a twelve-year-old boy in Cleveland, Ohio, the death of a forty-three-year-old man from a chokehold applied by a police officer in New York City, and all of these only in 2014. There have been many more such cases, culminating most recently with the death of George Floyd in May 2020 in Minneapolis, Minnesota.

Quite apart from the issue of police brutality, this brings to the fore the issue of racism and racial discrimination in the US. Because in all the above instances the victims were black and the police officers white. However, the explanations (or solutions, if you like), as most people will argue, are not so simple. But before that, let us understand that in India discrimination is not about race alone—in fact, it is even more complicated. India grapples with gender prejudice, caste prejudice and religious prejudice, at the very least.

Despite their complex nature, economics, without going into the historical and cultural antecedents, provides us two very simple and adequate notions of discrimination—statistical discrimination and taste-based discrimination—and they offer different explanations for the phenomenon of discrimination. For example, if we compare the above deaths to the behaviour of the Alabama police officer who pushed down and grievously injured the fifty-seven-year-old Sureshbhai Patel from Gujarat in India, do these incidents have the same explanation? Is it true that the same type of discrimination can be used to explain the death of George Floyd and the fact that African-American drivers are more likely to be stopped by the police?

Statistical Discrimination

The idea of statistical discrimination is usually credited to the Nobel Prize–winning economist, Kenneth Arrow. It says, statistically speaking, if an individual of one racial type (say, type M) is more likely to be involved in a criminal incident than an individual of another racial type (say, type N), then, when a police officer encounters a type M individual, the officer is more likely to have a prior belief that he is dealing with a criminal. Consequently, a police officer is more likely to stop such a person for a traffic infraction, more likely to search and investigate such an individual under suspicious conditions, and be more cautious and more likely to use force when dealing with this person.[1] It is also the same reason why a person who appears to be of West Asian origin may be subject to extra scrutiny at an airport.

This phenomenon arises when people use aggregate group characteristics, such as group averages or, for that matter, stereotypes, to evaluate individual (personal) characteristics. Then people belonging to different groups may be treated differently even if they are identical in every other aspect. Although, the original idea relies on observable characteristics of groups like race and gender, one can extend it to information and beliefs too; examples abound around us. Imagine an employer considering a male and a female individual for the same job. If they find out that the female just got married, they might worry that she will get pregnant at some point in the future. Even though it is not supposed to influence their decision, it might very well, and in some instances it probably does. Similarly, when a patient who is being happily treated in a hospital in India suddenly discovers that their doctor is a member of a socio-economically challenged scheduled caste, they might start entertaining thoughts/doubts about the doctor's ability. I have

---

[1]   It is worth reiterating that Arrow was not delving into what leads to this type of discrimination. He was merely trying to explain a phenomenon that we observe around us. One can imagine that stereotyping is a very complex social phenomenon. Let me illustrate in a very simple manner: crime is often associated with poverty. However, since a higher proportion of African-Americans are poorer, you might associate them with more criminal activity. This stereotyping does not take into account the history of slavery and unequal opportunities for the African-American population and is certainly not borne out by the arrest numbers for adults in the US population according to the US Department of Justice.

heard stories from my physician friends about how African-American doctors have a hard time being accepted as the person who is qualified to treat the patients.

Unfortunately, there is another very serious indirect consequence of judging an individual using group characteristics. Imagine that you belong to the group that is being discriminated against in the labour market. For instance, consider the following hypothetical scenario: If your first name is Sudipta then you will be discriminated against in the job market for economists. Armed with this fact, what will a rational Sudipta do? He will not bother to invest a lot in improving his economic skills because he will never earn enough to make up for the cost of acquiring these extra skills. In turn, this will reinforce what the employers already think about economists with the first name Sudipta. Thus, statistical discrimination will become a self-fulfilling outcome!

Of course, while statistical discrimination does not justify discriminatory behaviour against a particular individual, it relies on data—which creates certain beliefs based on which the officers in our examples may have a reason to behave in a certain way in order to ensure their own safety as well as the safety of others.[2] Sadly, it is something that individuals who are not prejudiced and rational can end up engaging in!

Taste-based Discrimination

Taste-based discrimination, propounded by the 1992 Nobel laureate Gary Becker, on the other hand, is based on the idea

---

[2] Of course, based on all the video evidence that is emerging, in many instances it requires a fairly elastic and stretchable imagination to believe the claims being put forward by the police officers.

that the members of a majority or influential group treat the members of the minority or less influential group unfavourably. Applied to the above situation, taste-based discrimination argues that an African-American individual is more likely to be treated with excessive force by the police simply because of their skin colour and not because they are more likely to be involved in a crime. And quite possibly an Indian man might face police brutality simply because he is Indian! Closer home, this would imply that the upper castes treat the lower castes unfavourably simply because of caste prejudice.

As the name suggests, this notion implies that an employer does not care about productivity and will not hire someone simply because they are biased or prejudiced against them and just do not want them around. Unlike statistical discrimination, it is not a rational action derived from certain criteria about the group but is just driven by taste or preferences; as such, it is hard to provide any kind of justification for taste-based discrimination. It is like my attitude to broccoli—I know broccoli is good for me, but I hate the taste and will not eat it even if someone paid me to do so![3] *Notice that in this instance the employer does not even care that they are losing out on productivity.* What does it imply for the group facing taste-based discrimination? Unfortunately, if you belong to the group facing discrimination, you may have

---

[3]   It is also necessary to point out that tastes typically do not arise in a vacuum—cultural conditioning and history play a big role. Possibly, I detest broccoli because growing up, I had never eaten broccoli—a vegetable that did not grow in India in those days. Similarly, there are plenty of Americans (the most famous one being George Bush) that hate broccoli because their parents forced them to eat it when they were children. Therefore, just like statistical discrimination, taste-based discrimination is also a complex social phenomenon.

to work harder for the same wages or possibly accept a lower wage for the same work relative to other employees—a fact that many people who face discrimination based on their skin colour, gender, sexual orientation, religion or caste can easily relate to.

One Key Difference

There is one key difference between statistical discrimination and taste-based discrimination in terms of how they manifest themselves. This relates to the notion of unconscious bias or implicit bias. This is typically defined as having unfounded judgements in favour of or against a person or a group relative to another, in a way that may be considered unfair. Research suggests that unconscious bias occurs automatically as the brain makes quick judgements based on past experiences and background. Clearly, you can have unconscious bias when you are engaging in taste-based discrimination. This possibility can also occur when we have statistical discrimination. And I can vouch for the fact that it does happen. I have been in meetings where I am the only non-white person in the room. I can also vouch for the fact that they are all well-meaning people. At times, if several people, including me, wish to ask a question or make a comment, I am usually the last person to get the chance to speak. Thus, unconscious bias manifests itself in subtle ways even with such well-meaning people.

In the Labour Market

Taste-based discrimination makes very stark predictions about the labour market. It says that African-American workers will receive a negative premium—that is, a African-American worker with the same productivity and ability as a white worker will have to accept a lower wage than their white counterpart in order to get an identical job.

In an influential study published in the *American Economic Review*, economists Marianne Bertrand and Sendhil Mullainathan sent identical fictitious résumés in response to help-wanted ads in Boston and Chicago newspapers.[4] Their results, though striking, were not unexpected: A white-sounding name (like Greg or Emily) as opposed to a black-sounding one (like Jamal and Lakiesha) received 50 per cent more callbacks for an interview!

What Happens in India . . .

In a similar study, the same authors along with Abhijit Banerjee (who won the Nobel Prize in 2019) and Saugato Datta sent identical fictitious résumés in response to 371 software and call-centre job openings advertised in newspapers and online job websites in and around Delhi. There are very few countries that are as diverse as India in terms of caste, language and religion. Since the operating language in these jobs is English, they did not focus on the language dimension. Their study focused on caste and religion. Perhaps in an India that is becoming more polarized by the day, these results will be weaker now, but their findings are certainly reassuring. The authors found that while there was no evidence of discrimination against scheduled castes (SC), scheduled tribes (ST) and other backward castes (OBC) for software jobs, non-upper-caste members (SC, ST and OBC) were found to be at a disadvantage for call-centre jobs. Also

---

[4]   The fact that the résumés were identical is to ensure that we do not have to contend with a possible statistical discrimination confound.

notable was the finding that Muslims are not systematically discriminated against in either of the two sectors. The authors concluded that overall there was no evidence that a candidate's caste mattered for interview callbacks. These findings are somewhat encouraging—it seems that credible skill certification, which is possible for software jobs (but not for call-centre jobs), reduces gaps in job opportunities. Thus, the observed discrimination seems to be statistical and not taste- or preference-based.

Discrimination of any form is a complex social problem and there are no easy solutions. Caste-based discrimination in India at least, it seems, can be eliminated by providing skill certification. And this might be the lesson—education which in the words of Professor Menah Pratt-Clarke can help us 'learn and unlearn ways of being', and widespread awareness may be our most viable solution. The time for action is now: universities need to get into this battle with everything they have!

Capturing Indian 'Crab' Behaviour

A few years ago, someone told me a story about an Indian businessman who made big bucks exporting crabs in containers with no lids. A cost-conscious rival who just couldn't bear the suspense finally asked the gentleman crab-exporter how he managed to export his crabs in lidless containers. Didn't those crustaceans simply crawl out and away?

Pat came the response: These were Indian crabs. The exporter did not have to worry about them escaping because the moment one crab tried climbing up, the others would pull him down. So long as he ensured the crabs were Indian, the exporter did not have to spend on lids for the containers. The savings from that were apparently significant enough, especially in a business where incremental cost advantages mattered. I cannot vouch for the story's veracity, but crabs pulling each other down is definitely a powerful metaphor for what is often touted as a very typical Indian trait—of not letting others forge ahead. Forget helping each other, Indians are apparently predisposed to even pulling others down at the slightest hint of their doing better.[1]

---

[1] My personal opinion on this keeps shifting. I have frequently experienced the kindness of strangers. However, this observation is neither about generosity/kindness and nor does it claim that Indians do not help each other. It is about how Indians would behave with each other in a rat race—say, in the fiercely competitive corporate

This did raise a different question for me, though. What if our gentleman exported say crabs from Sri Lanka and India together and put them in the same lidless container? Would the Indian crabs pull any crustacean trying to escape down or would they only do that to their own kind? Next, consider a two-state situation: What if the Indian crabs consisted of some Mallu and some Odia crabs? Imagine now that an Odia and a Mallu crab were trying to escape simultaneously. What would the other Odia crabs do? Pull down the Odia crustacean first?

Why Are We Crabs, After All?

In casual conversations, jealousy is put forward as the standard motive for the above-mentioned behaviour. However, I am not sure that this may be the only, or even the most likely, explanation. One can examine the crab problem from two different viewpoints:

- The first is whether this has to do with Indians primarily caring about how they are doing relative to others—the jealousy-type argument. Alternatively, we can put it in terms of the 'misery loves company' type argument: if you are not being successful, you do not want the others to succeed either.
- The second is whether they engage in such behaviour, not because of any concern over how others are doing, but because of the possibility of it adversely affecting their own

world of banking or Fast-Moving Consumer Goods (FMCGs). Unfortunately, I have yet to reach a verdict on this.

well-being. So this is not an argument about relative well-being or jealousy.

I will start with providing two explanations that seem to vindicate the 'relative-outcomes' argument put forward in the first bullet point. Such an argument applies very well to countries with high ethnic, linguistic or religious heterogeneity.

In general, I will argue that the more heterogeneous a society is, the higher are the efforts by people of one group to pull down those of the others. Research indicates that this is indeed true.

What exactly does it mean when we say that a society is heterogeneous and how would we measure this diversity? One way to capture it is by using an ethnolinguistic fractionalization index, that is, measuring the probability that two persons drawn at random from a country's population will not belong to the same ethnolinguistic group. One such exercise, carried out in the early 2000s by Harvard economist Alberto Alesina and his colleagues, developed three separate measures capturing such heterogeneity based on ethnicity, language and religion. For India, the corresponding index values were 0.418, 0.806 and 0.326.[2] What

---

[2] To get some perspective on this, let us consider the ethnicity index. Typically, African countries made up of different tribes are at the top and Uganda had the highest rank. The probability that two random Ugandans will be from different ethnicities was 0.9. At the bottom are islands like Reunion Island, São Tomé and Principe. Though surprisingly, this list also included Yemen. Interestingly, the number for the melting pot of the world, the United States, is 0.5 while for a homogenous country like Austria it is 0.1. Similar patterns that conform to our intuition can be found for the other two variables. Of course, one could argue that in India we should possibly look at caste, but there is no data on this.

does this tell us about India? Basically, that the highest diversity was in language—the probability of any two Indians drawn randomly from its large population not having the same linguistic background is 0.806—whereas heterogeneity along community and religion lines wasn't as marked.

Now, for my two explanations. The first assumes Odia crabs will not pull down one another, just as Malayali crabs surely wouldn't do this to their own brethren. They will just go for the other type—formally speaking, this is usually presented as an in-group, out-group phenomenon.[3] In fact, research published by economists Yan Chen and Sherry Li in the *American Economic Review* using American subjects shows that when matched with an in-group member, there is a 47 per cent increase in charitable desire. Compared to an out-group member, envy decreases by 93 per cent when matched with an in-group member. They also find that we are more likely to forgive an in-group member than an out-group member. In other words, our (favourable or positive) biases towards our own brethren are in some ways inherent. Another way to interpret this is—what may seem like deliberate nepotism is possibly an inherent or even an unconscious bias. Not that this subtle difference changes the outcome!

An alternative explanation supporting the relative-outcomes argument could be that people actually are more bothered about

---

[3] One issue with using the in-group, out-group taxonomy is that we have to broaden the scope of our thinking, i.e., we may have to go beyond envy as far as emotions go. We have to allow for things like anger and frustration. For instance, there might be anger against one group that gets jobs at the cost of another. A classic example is a group of upper caste people at dinner (the in-group) pointing to affirmative action or reservations in jobs for other castes (the out-group) as to what is wrong with the economy. This is quite possibly more than just envy.

how those from within their circles, as opposed to outsiders, are doing. In that case, it is the felt need to 'keep up with the Singhs' that pushes them to emulate, if not surpass, the attainment levels of their cohorts. And the envy stemming from not succeeding on that count, in turn, induces crab-like behaviour. For example, visualize middle-class parents in a large apartment complex in urban India comparing their own kids to the kids of other residents. In this battle for one-upmanship, everything goes: from praising one's own kid to taking insidious shots at the other kids. However, I seriously doubt whether this can be seen only as an Indian trait. People in many other parts of the world (especially in Asia) would/can also, perhaps, lay claim to this unenviable trait.

Crabs sans Envy

Next, instead of looking at arguments relying on relative differences to account for crab-like behaviour supposedly unique to Indians, one could also postulate *envy-free* explanations. This can arise from individuals simply caring about their own well-being, rather than comparing themselves with others—be it insiders or outsiders. Imagine, for instance, a team in which every single member has a specialized skill complementing that of the others, with each of these separate skills jointly contributing to the success of the team. This creates a situation where the team just cannot afford losing any member (remember Michael Kremer's O-ring theory). So, if a certain member of the group starts climbing up—by doing better in life—the sheer anxiety of that individual's exit pushes everyone to pull him down. In fact, I will go as far as to postulate that the force with which you are pulled down will be directly proportional to the value of your contribution to team output. Thus, it is not envy that induces the crab mentality, but a concern for *one's own well-being* arising from the possibility of reduced group performance!

Next, consider another scenario, where you have a group of friends from whom you seek help. If one or more of them plans to move elsewhere, it means a smaller friend circle to rely on and, hence, a lower probability of getting help. Another way of arguing the same is that if one of my friends starts doing well, he may not need me any more and, therefore, wouldn't be all that inclined to reciprocate and help me either in the future. While on the one hand I am happy for him, on the other hand, I am worried about him leaving. Suppose Mr Hyde wins this tug of war with Dr Jekyll, in my head. It, then, induces in me a desire to pull him down—back to my own level, where I will have peace of mind from the knowledge that he will continue to need my help. To use a nautical analogy, I want to scuttle his boat because I actually want him to help me when needed. That admittedly sounds incredulous, but my rejoinder to that would be that I am also game to go out on a fishing expedition with him when he wants me to. Thus, once again, it is not relative comparison, but an attempt to maximize one's own utility that can also lead to the Indian crab mindset.

Hopefully, these alternative explanations will help assuage the guilt of some who have pulled other crabs down!

Earthquake Economics

On 25 April 2015, Nepal was struck by an earthquake of
magnitude 7.8 on the Richter scale causing immense loss
of life and property. The aftershocks continued for quite a few
days. Although it will never be the same again for many people
and places, Nepal has returned to normality. The immediate
goal was to put the earthquake behind and move forward on
all fronts—I know this because my Nepali friends actually talk
about this earthquake in the past tense.

Earthquakes are not the only form of natural disaster.
We seem to be living in a time when both the magnitude
and frequency of natural disasters like cyclones, floods and
tsunamis seem to be increasing. In this essay, I want to examine
the relationship between catastrophic events and economic
behaviour, and though much of the analysis will carry over
to other natural disasters, I will restrict attention only to
earthquakes. This is partly to express solidarity towards my
Nepali friends and also because there is not a lot of research on
earthquakes in economics, making it easy for me to summarize it
in a short essay. Our friend Nejat Anbarci (at Deakin University
in Australia in 2015 and now at Durham University) and his
co-authors have been studying this particular type of natural
disaster for some time, and have come up with some absolutely
fascinating insights.

Human-Made Disasters

Natural disasters by themselves are non-discriminatory in nature—they do not engage in statistical or taste-based discrimination (see chapter titled 'Many Shades of Prejudice' for more on different types of discrimination that human beings are prone to). In other words, nature will not strike you more frequently simply because you were born in an earthquake-prone zone. Similarly, earthquakes do not preferentially target the prince or the pauper, or the Hindu or the Muslim. Yet the damage caused by disasters is not identical, and the prince and the pauper in general suffer its consequences differently.

My first-hand experience allows me to know this for a fact. In 2005, I was an assistant professor at Louisiana State University located in Baton Rouge, the capital of Louisiana, and an hour west of New Orleans. It was my first real experience of a hurricane: incessant rain, shrieking winds and the eerily calm eye of the storm—much like a cyclone in India. Except that the people of Louisiana had a very different attitude towards hurricanes. Apart from stocking up on bread, milk and water, they always stocked up on liquor. Initially, I was quite surprised and naturally wanted to know all about the stocked-up liquor. I was told, 'It is going to rain a lot, we will be stuck inside with probably no power. What else is there to do but drink?' Now, that is the spirit of Louisiana—home to generations of slaves, Cajuns who made a living from the marshy land and, very significantly, the birthplace of jazz. The state is quite different from the rest of the US. As they frequently say in Louisiana, '*les bons temps rouler*' or, let the good times roll—even if there is a hurricane round the corner.

When Hurricane Katrina hit New Orleans in 2005, the good times certainly did not roll through. The whole world has seen those shocking images of devastation and deprivation. But, it is the poor who suffered disproportionately more. Their homes were at a greater risk of flooding simply because they lived in neighbourhoods that were below sea level, like the Lower 9th Ward. I myself in Baton Rouge was without power for four days—while the richer parts of the city got it back earlier, power was returned to the poorer parts even later.

On the other hand, when Hurricane Gustav hit Baton Rouge (home to both of us) in 2008, the rich were at a disadvantage. There was no danger of floods in Baton Rouge. Most of the damage was due to falling trees caused by high winds, and the affluent lived in areas that tended to have greater number of trees than the poorer neighbourhoods. Consequently, their houses, their vehicles and the infrastructure in their area suffered greater damage—a rare instance where the prince was hit harder than the pauper. There is another important point to note here. If we were all cavemen, then an earthquake would affect everyone in the same manner. However, human activity or 'built infrastructure', a term much in use these days, makes places different, and fatalities caused by natural disasters therefore are also different.

Interestingly, when studying the factors that determine the impact of earthquakes using data at the country-level, my friend Nejat Anbarci and his co-authors have found that the fatalities caused by earthquakes are not only negatively related to income per capita, but are greater in countries with greater income inequality. Why is this? Because the ability of a country to reach an agreement on how resources must be allocated for mitigating fatalities caused by earthquakes is positively associated with income equality. Hence, in countries with high income inequality, the rich can insure themselves against earthquakes, leaving the poor vulnerable.

Thus, while nature does not discriminate, human activity leads to differential impacts on the rich and the poor.

Agents of Change

Destructive as they may be, economists also view natural disasters as a window of opportunity—the opportunity to rebuild. Earthquakes are no exception. By destroying the existing infrastructure, they create a necessity to replace these with new and improved (seismic-resistant, for example) ones. In this sense, earthquakes can be thought of as providing 'creative destruction', in the words of the great economist Joseph Schumpeter.

While in the short run creative destruction may cause considerable economic suffering, in the long run it produces substantial economic benefits for the society as a whole. In fact, research using country-level data shows that in the long run *earthquakes affect income positively*. This was also found to be true in a study using household-level data from Indonesia—a country that frequently experiences earthquakes as it sits at the intersection of several tectonic plates. A simple way to understand this is that an earthquake provides the opportunity to replace crumbling infrastructure with more efficient things— like better roads and bridges or better electric wiring, which in turn lead to higher productivity and incomes.[1]

---

[1] The idea, of course, is old enough to appear in the Mahabharata. Agni's destruction of the Khandava forest allows Agni to regain his strength and lustre, and also facilitates the construction of the city of Indraprastha.

Earthquakes and Politics

Earthquakes not only reshape the topography of an area, but they also have the potential to reshape political and democratic institutions. Research by Anbarci and his co-authors shows that the effect of earthquakes on political transitions is not very straightforward—there are both direct and indirect effects. Earthquakes directly affect the re-election chances of an incumbent government since the public might hold them responsible for all the damages. A severe earthquake also causes economic stress in the short run, making it easier to bring about a political regime change when such forces exist. Additionally, the distribution of massive amount of resources for recovery and development among different groups and constituencies can also create discontented groups. Such groups then are likely to vote against the government in an upcoming election. Thus, the direct effect of an earthquake is pro-democratic. However, research also shows that earthquakes may affect political institutions indirectly through their (indirect) positive impacts on incomes in the long run. This can serve to make an existing government more autocratic since it becomes difficult for the Opposition to fight an incumbent government that can demonstrate significant economic progress.

Earthquake Relief

We are human beings and we do care about other fellow beings in distress. The Nepal earthquake made this very clear. The international community, including India, was quick to show support. Relief came in the form of emergency supplies, troops and medical aid. In addition to this, several countries and NGOs provided millions of dollars, with the UN contributing about $15 million. One question that economists have pondered over is what affects the flow of relief. Would a country other than Nepal have received more or less in terms of relief aid?

Research shows that the amount of disaster relief depends on a number of factors, including the colonial history of the affected country, whether it shares a common language with the donor countries and engages in trade with them, whether or not it is a friend of the UN, and the distance between the disaster-affected country and the donor country. Interestingly, it turns out that to receive the same level of disaster relief, a country with no colonial ties must experience fifty times more fatalities than a former colony. So whatever other consequences colonial ties might have had, when it comes to disaster relief, the shared past does have a positive impact.

Corruption and Earthquakes

The real question in the context of disaster relief, however, is not how much relief was received, but what proportion actually made it to the affected population. It is a serious issue in developing countries with high-levels of corruption and notoriously leaky government-controlled distribution channels. In fact, it has been suggested that corruption was one of the major causes behind the high fatality rate of the 1999 Odisha supercyclone.

In the context of earthquakes, however, public sector corruption can have serious impact through another channel. Death tolls caused by earthquakes can be higher because corruption makes it possible to ignore building codes, which ultimately magnify the severity of earthquakes leading to more deaths and a greater loss of property. According to Anbarci's study, an earthquake of similar magnitude will kill more than twice as many people in India as it would in Australia, simply because of differences in the levels of corruption. India's average corruption scores for the study period (1997–2003) is 3.3 and Australia's is 6—a higher number implies lower corruption. Of course, if this carries over to the infrastructure sector, then when aftershocks rumble through the earthquake zone for days on end, as they did in Nepal, further damage to life and property will keep occurring, making it difficult to restore normalcy for quite some time.

The original version of this piece was written for The Hindu BusinessLine *with my former PhD student and co-author Dr Chandan Jha. So the 'we' here refers to him and is not an attempt by me to confer royalty status on myself.*

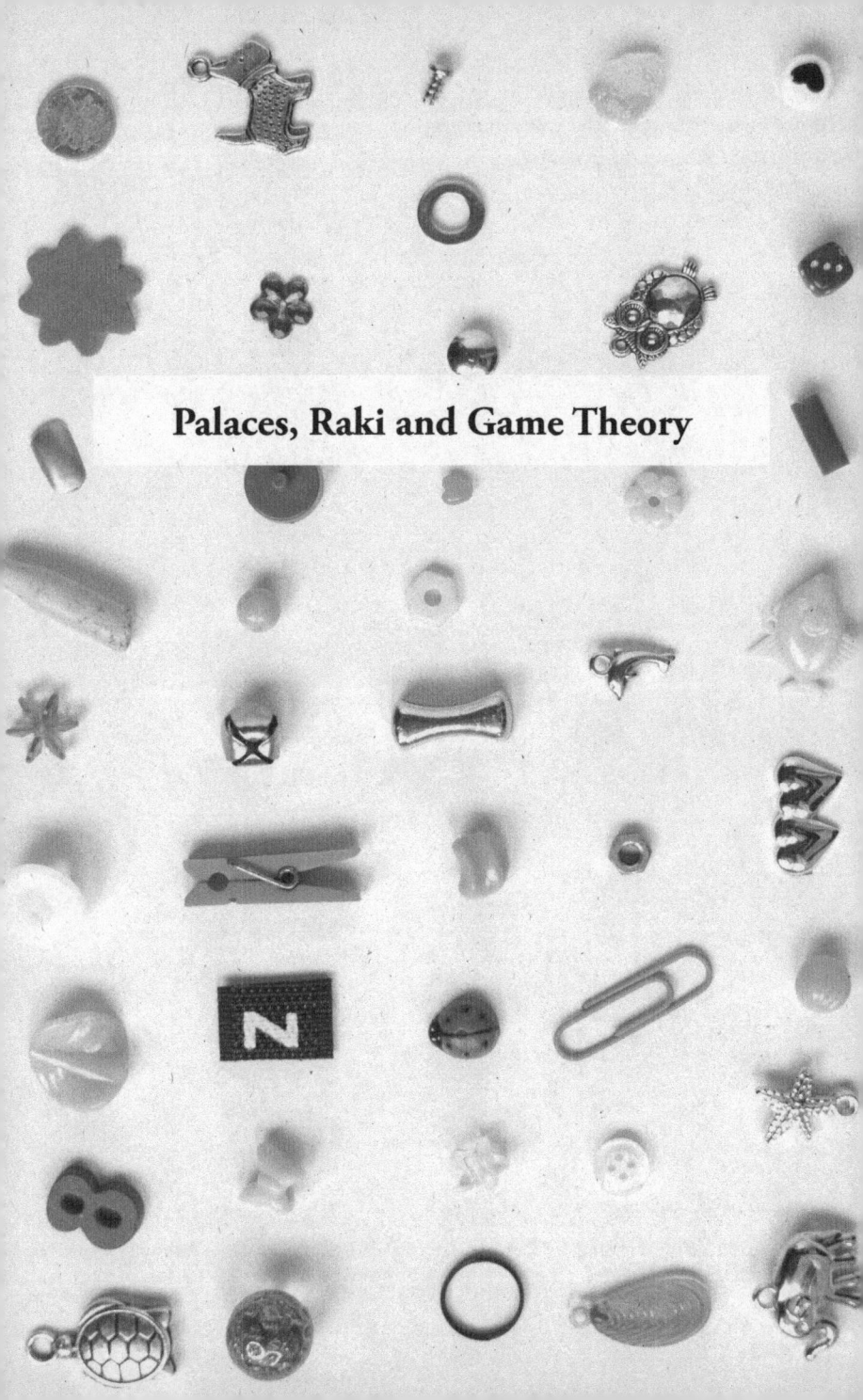

Palaces, Raki and Game Theory

This piece is as much about travel in Turkey as about economics. So I have taken the liberty of allowing myself a few byzantine detours.

It was the summer of 2012. I was in the wonderful city of Istanbul, the venue of the Fourth World Congress of the Game Theory Society (aka Games 2012). Just like the Olympics, this is an event held every four years and is, in fact, sometimes referred to as the Game Theory Olympics—even though there are no medals to be awarded. Not surprisingly, it draws in those working in game theory and related areas from all over the world. The tag line for the conference, hosted by Bilgi University, was '*Istanbul Welcomes Beautiful Minds*'. That was an obvious reference to the four Nobel Prize winners—Eric Maskin, Roger Myerson, Reinhard Selten and, of course, the original beautiful mind, John Forbes Nash, Jr. They were all going to be talking at this conference.

Detour #1: Nobel Prize Winners in Game Theory

Both Eric Maskin, who is at Harvard, and Roger Myserson, who is at the University of Chicago, won the Nobel Prize for economics (along with Leonid Hurwicz) in 2007 for 'having laid the foundations of mechanism design theory' according to the Nobel Foundation's press release. Mechanism design helps economists distinguish between situations in which markets work well from those in which they do not, especially in the absence of full or complete information about everyone involved in the problem. It plays a key role in many areas of economics, computer science and political science. Examples include identifying efficient trading mechanisms, regulatory schemes and voting procedures. Incidentally, following the notion of the Erdös number, I am happy to report that in the co-authorship network of economists, I am at a distance of 3 from Professor Eric Maskin and 4 from Professor Roger Myserson. A distance of 3 means that I have written a paper with someone (Myrna Wooders, Vanderbilt) who has written a paper with someone (Peter Hammond, Warwick) who has written a paper with Eric Maskin.

John Nash Jr and Reinhard Selten received the Nobel Prize for economics in 1994 'for their pioneering analysis of equilibria in the theory of non-cooperative games'. According to the Nobel Foundation's press release, John Nash Jr formulated how to find the equilibrium of a simultaneous-move game (like Rock-Paper-Scissors), which is now eponymously called a Nash equilibrium. It is a situation from which no one wishes to deviate unilaterally, i.e., if everyone else is driving on the left-hand side of the road, then you do not wish to be the only one driving on the right. In that sense, it is stable, and therefore an equilibrium of the game. Professor Nash also laid the foundations of bargaining theory, all in his twenty-six-page dissertation with a bibliography consisting of two references. Professor Reinhard Selten extended this to sequential-move games (like Tic-Tac-Toe or chess). His idea was that the equilibrium of such a game, called the *Subgame Perfect Nash Equilibrium*, requires that you must be playing a Nash equilibrium in every stage of the game, given the history of the game. In other words, at any stage of the game, the player(s) involved in that stage must be playing a Nash equilibrium given what has happened in the game till then.

Now, imagine attending a full day of meetings where such concepts and their refinements are being thrown at you constantly. It can be mind-numbing and exhausting! After four days of four plenary sessions, four semi-plenary sessions and 498 invited papers, well, you'll certainly start getting a hang of what's happening at the frontiers of game-theory research. The conference covered all the usual suspects like evolutionary games, mechanism design and contract theory, social choice, voting, and political economy. But two emerging areas that seemed to receive special emphasis were algorithmic game theory and networks.

New Games

Algorithmic game theory, as some researchers in the field put it, is the confluence of two ideas put forth by the great Hungarian-American mathematician, John von Neumann: Game theory and algorithms. Game theory basically looks at how human beings behave in situations where the final outcome depends on the actions of more than one person, as in a game of chess or Tic-Tac-Toe. An algorithm is a finite and precise set of instructions to achieve a certain desired outcome. In algorithmic game theory, the objective, then, is to design algorithms for particular strategic situations, based on predictions of human behaviour provided by game theory, and to achieve the desired outcomes algorithmically. The beauty of this approach lies in the fact that algorithms behave like the true *Homo economicus*—the perfectly rational agents whose existence is usually assumed by economic theory. There were a number of related papers at the conference focusing on the complexity of obtaining computational solutions to game-theoretic problems in domains such as logistics. Not surprisingly, we had the normal slew of papers on auctions and mechanism design—major areas of interest to game theorists and computer scientists alike.

The study of networks and its applications in economics is about twenty years old now. An excellent introduction can be found in Stanford professor Matthew Jackson's recent book titled *The Human Network*. In contrast to the research on this subject in sociology and physics, the first question economists seek to ask is how human networks are formed in the first place. The typical set-up is as follows: Imagine a set of individuals deciding who to establish links or relationships with. Establishing links with others confers benefits but is costly to do so. The framework can then make assumptions about how information flows in the networks—sometimes it may be deterministic but at other times it may be probabilistic, that is, some relationships may work probabilistically. It is a bit like saying that you make a phone call but there is only a certain probability that you will reach the intended person and get the necessary information from them. In the deterministic case, you always find the person you are looking for, perhaps simply because you access their web page and are not trying to reach them by phone. How do you deal with information decay, i.e., information coming through several intermediaries, is less valuable than information directly from the source or those close to the source?

Questions of interest may be: What is the role of incentives in the formation of networks and do networks that are stable from an individual's perspective coincide with the ones that are socially optimal? While some papers at the conference examined how people learn from their neighbours and how influence spreads in a network, others looked at institutions that impose constraints on local interactions and who can link with whom. There was also a selection of papers offering insights on the role of social networks in influencing bargaining, besides the disruption of networks caused by the exit of players. My favourite paper was the one on how people bond together when facing a common enemy.

Ottoman Models

But even better, if not the best thing, that the conference had to offer was Istanbul itself. Spread across two continents, this is a city steeped in history and culture. The sweltering July heat during the day was, no doubt, exhausting, but as the locals say, when the sun sets, even the most harassed traveller will forget all the day's misadventures and embrace the city with open arms.

The cool sea breeze, night views of the Bosporus strait, the mezze plate with numerous hot and cold offerings, fresh seafood under the Galata Bridge, endless varieties of local kebabs, raki (Turkish arrack) and mouth-watering desserts—I can fill an entire page with descriptions of just those. Besides the Bosporus that separates the Asian and European parts of the city, there is also an estuary called the Golden Horn dividing old and new Istanbul. The Bosporus and the Golden Horn converge towards the Sea of Marmara, on which a bevy of boats, ferries and ships—large, small and just as numerous as the fish in the water—operate.

Detour #2: Raki

No write-up about a visit to Turkey can be complete without raki (pronounced *ra'kw* and derived from the Arabic word arak). Raki is a clear, somewhat sweet, aniseed-flavoured liquor (generally about 90 per cent proof) and is considered to be the national drink of Turkey. Versions of this drink are popular in the neighbouring countries as well: the Greeks have ouzo and the Italians have grappa. Once you add water to raki (this is how it is usually drunk), it turns white and hence the nickname '*aslansütü*' or lion's milk. It is not a drink for everyone—only the brave and strong. Drinking raki usually requires a group of good friends and plenty of food, especially cheese (*peynir* in Turkish) and kebabs, and the circle that is formed is the equivalent of the Indian adda. So gather up a bunch of friends, order plenty of food, eat a bit and raise a toast (*şerefe* in Turkish) and take a sip; no bottoms up here—you definitely nurse your drink! In fact, it is believed that Atatürk, the founder of modern Turkey, is supposed to have said, 'The best accompaniment to raki is good conversation.'

And now back to old Istanbul.

Old Istanbul reminds you of Old Delhi with stunning examples of Ottoman architecture—the magnificent Topkapi Palace, the Sultan Ahmed mosque with its beautiful blue tiles, the Hagia Sophia (a church that became a mosque and is now a museum), the New Mosque (that was actually completed in 1665) and the Grand Bazaar, which is somewhat like our own Chandni Chowk.

While the typical Ottoman architecture is a blend of Byzantine and Islamic styles, my personal favourite was the Dolmabahçe Palace, built on the Bosporus in the latter half of the Ottoman rule, incorporating both Baroque and Rococo elements. Note that this palace is built with wood. Hence, for preservation reasons, there is a limit on the number of visitors that can be inside the building at any given time. So if you plan to visit this magnificent edifice, make sure that you either arrive there early, or late—it will help you avoid long waiting lines (there was no higher priced VIP line engaging in price discrimination when I was last there). As you take the guided tour through the palace, you are stunned not only by its gilded splendour but also the constant footfalls and whispers that rustle through the corridors. In the hot, heavy and still July air, you get a feel for the conspiracies and court intrigues that a dying empire would have witnessed.

Quite a lot of game theory there.

Facebook against Corruption

In December 2010, a wave of powerful protests erupted in many Arab countries. Now termed as the Arab Spring, this tumultuous event really shook the world. It saw ordinary people take to the streets to fight against oppressive regimes on the strength of mere human spirit. The Arab Spring led to the demise of many dictatorships, including those in Egypt, Libya, Tunisia and Yemen. Other countries, like Bahrain and Syria, observed serious civil uprisings; even Iraq, Jordan and Kuwait did not escape turmoil.

Fast forward to 2011, a protest, led by the social activist, Anna Hazare, shook India. This time, the protest was against corruption. Millions of people, primarily the youth that were fed up with corruption scandals making headlines on a regular basis in India, joined the protest at Jantar Mantar in New Delhi. The protest was so successful that one of the key lieutenants of Anna Hazare, Arvind Kejriwal, was able to become (and continues to be) the chief minister of Delhi by forming a new political party with a primarily anti-corruption agenda. In fact, *Time* magazine featured these protests as one of the top-ten stories of the year.

Why Social Media?

Social media had a significant role to play in the success of these movements by providing (i) a means for rapid communication,

(ii) unique opportunities for interaction among the protestors and (iii) a personal touch. As I learned from a colleague of mine, the recent protests in Hong Kong did indeed rely on these three aspects: there was no single leader driving the movement. Social media provided a platform where group discussions drove decisions regarding the protests by a large group of people. Moreover, social media platforms ensure rapid communication that can simultaneously reach a large group, allowing protesters to be agile and stay ahead of their rivals. Prior to the Arab Spring, given the sheer gap between the ruling elites and the lay public, political pundits in Egypt were anticipating street discontent. It is social media that accelerated this process. In Tunisia, the social networking sites actually provided the initial spark by allowing for quick dissemination of information and feedback. As an Egyptian protestor succinctly summarized it, 'We use Facebook to schedule the protests, Twitter to coordinate and YouTube to tell the world.'

In India as well, social media was arguably the key ingredient in the success of the anti-corruption movement: it was hardly a secret that young India, with a greater exposure to the world (made possible by both technology and improvements in education facilities), was frustrated with corruption and willing to act on it. The organizers and the supporters of the movement took advantage of this knowledge to connect easily and quickly with like-minded people, and to coordinate about the venue and timing of the protest for maximum visibility and impact. Finally, the large user base of social media implied a bigger audience with whom news regarding corruption could be shared rapidly.

For organizing a protest, what is even more important is the source of information: on social media platforms, a large fraction of our friends are typically people we know very well and this adds a personal touch to all aspects of the information. Such information from an acquaintance is perceived to be more reliable, and the users also feel compelled to act on it in some way to show solidarity to their loved ones.

Street Games

The foundational blueprint for such protests is the same: Protestors basically create event/action pages on Facebook and Twitter on the basis of some sort of consensus in a core group. Once the relevant information is put in the public domain on social networking sites, the 'snowball effect' does the rest: People share the events with their family members and acquaintances, who further share these with their relatives and acquaintances, and so on. Occasional 'personal' video footage of police or military atrocities add spice to the mix. Such crowd-sourced information incited the sort of rage that fuelled the Arab Spring.

Social media abetted these uprisings, essentially by creating what game theorists call 'focal points', a notion for which Thomas Schelling received the Nobel Prize in economics in 2005. Simply put, focal points can help one select between multiple optimal solutions—and therefore can assist in resolving coordination problems. Why do many airports designate a spot as the Meeting Point? This is done so that even complete strangers who are meeting for the first time (for instance, for a hotel pick-up) and have no mobile phones can just choose to go there without worrying about the multiple meeting location possibilities provided by the airport. Actually, just being aware that the Meeting Point exists eliminates the need to fix a meeting place in advance. Focal points are driven by things like culture. For example, people from Japan choose to drive on the left, while people from France will choose to drive on the right, even if no one tells them to. Focal points may be driven by a shared context, like two Harry Potter fans naturally gravitating to the wall labelled Platform 9¾ at the Charring Cross Station in London. Of course, they may be also exogenously created, like Meeting Points in airports and train stations. Regardless, Schelling's idea was that focal points help choose between multiple (Nash) equilibria of the game and if one does not exist, it might be a good idea to create spaces like Meeting Points. Social media played the key role of naming designated locations—focal points—where protestors could show up in large numbers, instead of undertaking fragmented demonstrations. And this was crucial for the Arab Spring, Anna Hazare's India Against Corruption (IAC) movement and, more recently, for the protests in Hong Kong.

Deterrent Effect

While the contribution of social media in dislodging or undermining entrenched Arab dictatorships is well-recognized, has this virtual platform been really able to fight corruption as well? Can we really think of Facebook against Corruption? To answer this, we decided to investigate the impact of Facebook usage on corruption across countries. The idea was simple: In any country with a large number of Facebook users, news regarding graft can be spread easily and quickly. That, in turn, can have a deterrent effect, especially in urban areas—recall the Anna movement's use of Facebook to create awareness about corruption and organize protest events. We collected data on both corruption and Facebook usage for over 150 countries from around the world. Data on corruption was obtained from Transparency International, a leading NGO that publishes corruption indices for countries, using inputs from sources such as the Asian Development Bank, African Development Bank, Freedom House and the World Bank.

Our findings did, indeed, reveal a significant, negative correlation between Facebook usage and corruption. Simple regression analysis further confirmed that higher Facebook usage is associated with lower levels of corruption. To make our findings robust, we added a number of additional variables like education and income levels for each country to the regression and found that our results persisted. Note that these additional control variables are important since it allows us to put all countries on the same level, facilitating an apples to apples comparison (and not apples to oranges!).

Interestingly, complementarity also shows up here. We found that the correlation between social media and corruption is stronger in countries where the press enjoys greater freedom. Imagine two countries—one where the press is perceived to be independent and free from government control and the other where the press is under government control and considered 'not free'. Then social media will have a greater effect on corruption in the first country because of two possible reasons. First, social media can be used to disseminate unbiased news regarding corruption. Second, individuals are more likely to act on such unbiased news.

It is also worth keeping in mind that the role of social media in lowering corruption may be much bigger than what we found (think about Chinese microbloggers—their impact on the government's operations may not be small). In other words, in the countries we study, there may not be enough people speaking English (Facebook's lingua franca) or having Internet access at all. Once we eliminate these issues, the effect will probably be larger.

Secrecy in Graft

Petty corruption by its very nature is different from major political scams and creates a different type of interaction which, in turn, can limit what organized protests and social media can do to address it. It requires only a few leaders to organize political protests and social media can quickly spread the message. Moreover, event pages can be created anonymously on Facebook. Graft, on the other hand, does not always indicate large scams. Much of it actually is of a petty nature, though massive when we add it all up. Petty corruption occurs when one individual has regulatory authority over another. In these situations, most people will not report graft activities on social media sites, since both the bribe giver and the taker are deemed guilty. Reporting will not happen in the absence of substantial anonymity or privacy. This only reinforces the case for leniency towards bribe givers in petty corruption matters—a suggestion made by Professor Kaushik Basu, former chief economic advisor to the Government of India. While social media can help educate people about corruption and how to fight it, it will not have a substantial impact without an effective law protecting whistleblowers. Till then, the popular refrain that Facebook is only spoiling kids is likely to continue!

This chapter is based on a paper that I published with Chandan Jha.

Chicken: The Game Politicians Love to Play

The Game of Chicken is one politicians play frequently.[1] In fact, there is one being played on the global stage right now—the two players are the American President Donald Trump and Chinese President Xi Jinping. Sometime in 2018, Trump announced a series of tariffs on Chinese goods coming into the US and the Chinese retaliated. Over the course of the year, neither side backed down, negotiators were largely unsuccessful, and things have only escalated. It is also true that both economies are suffering because of this. This is the essence of a Game of Chicken—neither side wants to appear weak by being the first to back down, even when it is costly!

In recent years, as American politics has become more partisan, there have been many instances of the Game of Chicken. A common one that keeps recurring is the government shutdown over the budget. The Republicans and the Democrats fail to agree on passing the budget, leading typically to a partial federal government shutdown. When this happens, most 'non-essential' government services stand suspended. Thus, national parks are closed and passport applications go unprocessed. On

---

[1] Depending on your taste, you might first want to read the formal description of the Game of Chicken in game-theoretic terms and its Nash equilibrium in a separate section at the end of this chapter.

the other hand, military and police activities as well as certain other essential time-sensitive services—such as air traffic control and hurricane tracking—continue unhindered. Although not an ideal situation, overall, this has a relatively minor impact on the US economy. It has happened before, since the mid-1970s through the mid-1990s to several instances in recent years and will probably happen with greater frequency in the years to come.

However, the second issue over which Chicken can be played by the Republicans and Democrats is larger and more important. That issue is the showdown over the federal 'debt ceiling', and in recent years such a crisis happened in 2013.

The US Debt Ceiling

The US debt ceiling is the amount of debt that the US treasury is allowed by the Congress. This effectively limits the amount of money the federal government can borrow. The Congress has passed contradictory laws over the years, calling for certain levels of spending and taxation, while also imposing limits on how much debt the government can issue. In 2011, the limit on the national debt was set at $16.394 trillion, which was reached by the end of December 2012 and hence the crisis of 2013. At that point, if the Congress would not have raised the debt ceiling again, the US treasury department would have been left with several bad options.

Debt Ceiling: Some Non-Options

The first option was to prioritize the debt. This would possibly require continuing to make interest payments on

US treasury bonds. While this option would help prevent a collapse in bond markets, it would, however, also entail serious curtailing of spending elsewhere. The severity of such spending cuts could well push the US economy back into a recession. A second option, of defaulting on payments on treasuries, is of course a sure-shot recipe for chaos. The First Law of Bond Markets—if such a law were to exist—is that US treasury bonds carry zero risk of default. Violation of this would trigger panic selling and most likely cause widespread global economic disruption.

Other unusual options also exist. For example, the US treasury could use its power to mint coins, to issue currency of high face-value for financing ongoing government operations. Another option would be to simply declare that the debt limit, the tax code and the spending bills conflict with each other, making it impossible to follow all of them at once. This would then create 'reasonable grounds' for violating the existing debt limit. While these alternative options have some appeal, questions regarding their legitimacy (if they are ever invoked) will render their chances of success unlikely. In any case, they certainly won't help in calming the global bond markets.

Hollywood's Love Affair with Chicken

Given the non-options mentioned above, the debt-limit negotiations that took place in 2013 were essentially a high-stakes Game of Chicken. But politicians are not the only ones who love to play Chicken—Hollywood is the one who popularized this game! The most famous example is seen in the Hollywood classic, *Rebel without a Cause*. At some point in the movie, two drivers begin driving at high speeds towards the edge of a cliff. The one who panics and jumps out of the car *first* is the loser. The other driver, having proven himself to be braver by continuing to drive towards the cliff (though he, too, must eventually get out), earns the group's respect and the girl's love. However, the consequences would be disastrous if both drivers keep waiting for the other person to get out first and neither jumps. In that event, both go over the cliff: A dead driver does not live to tell any tales and is obviously not a winner.[2]

In terms of the formal description of Chicken at the end of this chapter, each driver has two strategies: either to jump out (Swerve) or keep driving (Don't Swerve). If one of them gets out while the other continues driving (the {S, DS} or the {DS, S} outcome), he loses the game and suffers loss of respect. The driver who keeps going gains respect and, hopefully, does not lose his life. If both jump out (the {S, S} outcome), it's like a tie: both lose an equal but small amount of respect. Clearly, playing the *Rebel without a Cause* version of Chicken would require that the players continue driving until the last possible moment, and then get out. However—as it always happens in Holly, Bolly or Tollywood—eventually, sleeves get caught, brakes fail and a whole host of other things play out in the last moment. The result is that only James (you

---

[2] The appeal of this game to Hollywood, beyond macho teenage boys believing themselves to be immortal, is the high danger involved. Without the possibility of a terrible end result, the game loses its appeal.

could easily substitute James Dean with Dharmendra or Rajnikanth) lives on.[3]

Rebels with Causes

Although they are not even rebels without causes, what transpired in Washington in 2013 was just a Game of Chicken being played between congressional leaders and President Barack Obama. The Republican Party, which had little leverage otherwise, was using the threat of not allowing a breach of the debt limit to force concessions on other legislations, to which they were hostile. Since Obama was committed to these other legislations, he was obviously unwilling to play ball (by swerving). The Republican side's reasoning was that breaching the debt limit was such a bad idea that Obama would blink first and agree to some concessions. Further complicating the situation, John Boehner and other Republican leaders were simultaneously playing an *internal* Game of Chicken with some extreme members of their own party, who were apparently more willing to risk default. Luckily, in the end, good sense prevailed and the debt ceiling was raised to $16.699 trillion.

No wonder the great philosopher Bertrand Russel said the following about politicians and the Game of Chicken:

---

[3] In fact, that is what happened to the big bad bully Buzz Gunderson (Corey Allen) in the movie—his sleeve got caught and he could not jump out!

Since the nuclear stalemate became apparent, the Governments of East and West have adopted the policy which Mr. Dulles[4] calls 'brinkmanship'. This is a policy adapted from a sport which, I am told, is practised by some youthful degenerates. This sport is called 'Chicken!' It is played by choosing a long straight road with a white line down the middle and starting two very fast cars towards each other from opposite ends. Each car is expected to keep the wheels on one side of the white line. As they approach each other, mutual destruction becomes more and more imminent. If one of them swerves from the white line before the other, the other, as they pass, shouts 'Chicken!', and the one who has swerved becomes an object of contempt. As played by irresponsible boys, this game is considered decadent and immoral, though only the lives of the players are risked. But when the game is played by eminent statesmen, who risk not only their own lives but those of many hundreds of millions of human beings, it is thought on both sides that the statesmen on one side are displaying a high degree of wisdom and courage, and only the statesmen on the other side are reprehensible. This, of course, is absurd. Both are to blame for playing such an incredibly dangerous game. The game may be played without misfortune a few times, but sooner or later it will come to be felt that loss of face

---

[4] Here, Russel is referring to John Foster Dulles who served as the Secretary of State under President Dwight Eisenhower from 1953 to 1958.

is more dreadful than nuclear annihilation. The moment will come when neither side can face the derisive cry of 'Chicken!' from the other side. When that moment is come, the statesmen of both sides will plunge the world into destruction.

I would like to dedicate this chapter to the late Dr Matt Wiser who used to teach at the University of South Alabama. He was the victim of a random robbery gone wrong and the ubiquitous presence of guns in America. An early version of this chapter was written with him.

Appendix 1: The Game of Chicken

The Story: Game theorists like telling simple stories to illustrate the idea behind games they analyse. The typical story associated with Chicken is the one made famous by the movie *Rebel without a Cause*. Two drivers race towards the edge of a cliff. The first one to swerve before reaching the end of the cliff is the loser. Of course, if they both do not swerve, then they will fall off the cliff. If they both serve, they both lose face, but will live to tell the tale. As we have already discussed, a slightly modified version was also proposed by Bertrand Russell.

Formal Description of the Game: Chicken is an example of what game theorists call a simultaneous move two-player game. The game has two players each with two strategies—Swerve (S) and Don't Swerve (DS). As opposed to a sequential move game, in this game both players must move simultaneously (like in Rock-Paper-Scissors), i.e., they must choose their strategies without knowing what the other player has chosen. Note that there are four possible outcomes in this game: they both swerve (S, S), both don't swerve (DS, DS) and the two asymmetric possibilities where one chooses swerve and the other chooses don't swerve: (S, DS) and (DS, S). The figure below represents this information in a matrix format that game-theorists typically use for such games along with the associated payoffs.

		Player 2	
Player 1		Swerve (**S**)	Don't Swerve (**DS**)
	Swerve (**S**)	2, 2	1, 3
	Don't Swerve (**DS**)	3, 1	0,0

As can be seen from the matrix, Player 1 is typically designated as the Row player and Player 2 the Column player. Next to each player are the two strategies they can choose—think of these as the two possible buttons, of which they must choose one without knowing what the other player has chosen. As already noted, the game allows for four possible outcomes and the numbers in each cell represent the payoffs of the two players from each outcome. The first number is Player 1's payoff and the second number is Player 2's payoff. So if both choose to swerve, then the outcome is (S,S) and they both get a payoff of 2. If Player 1 choses DS and Player 2 choses S, they end up in the bottom-left cell and Player 1 earns 3 while Player 2 earns 1. The top right has the opposite payoffs. If they do not swerve, the outcome is really bad and they both earn 0 each.

Finding the Nash Equilibrium: A Nash equilibrium, named after John Nash Jr, who won the Nobel Prize for economics in 1994, and on whose life the movie *A Beautiful Mind* is based, suggested a method to find the equilibrium or stable outcome of such games. Since this is a simultaneous move game, in an equilibrium, it follows that neither player should wish to change their strategy, given that the other player is sticking to their strategy, i.e., a Nash equilibrium is robust to 'unilateral deviation'—deviation by one person at a time. Thus, in a Nash equilibrium, each player is playing an optimal response (formally speaking—a best response) to the other player.

Now, let us apply this to the Game of Chicken. Clearly, (S,S) is not stable, because each player will be better off deviating to DS as long as the other player is playing S (unilateral deviation) and earning 3. Similarly, (DS, DS) is also not stable since each player is better off deviating to S since 1 is better than 0. Now, consider the situation (S, DS). As long as Player 2 will play DS, Player 1 cannot do better by playing DS since they will get 0 (the outcome will be [DS, DS]) instead of the current payoff of 2. From Player 2's perspective, as long as Player 1 is playing S, she cannot do better by switching to S unilaterally, since the outcome will move to (S, S) and she will earn 1 instead of 3. Thus, (S, DS) is a Nash equilibrium. Similar reasoning can be used to check that (DS, S) is also a Nash equilibrium. Thus, the Game of Chicken has two Nash equilibria: (S, DS) and (DS, S). This is intuitive since in both these Nash equilibria, one player would prefer not to swerve but would like the other player to swerve and be called Chicken.

Some Interesting Features of Chicken: The game of Chicken has some very interesting features. First, in this game, not being called Chicken is worth more than dying! This suggests that it is a game where reputation is worth more than life itself. In other words, if you cannot preserve your reputation or honour, life is not worth living. No wonder we find politicians and world leaders frequently playing this game. Without reputation, the chances of re-election go away—for instance, neither Indian nor Pakistani leaders, regardless of their personal opinions, can appear to be weak on Kashmir simply because it has serious re-election consequences. The same goes for the battle between Trump and Xi Jinping—neither can back out from the fight.

Another interesting feature is that there are two asymmetric Nash equilibria (not on the main diagonal of the matrix, but in the top-left and bottom-right corners) in this game. In terms of actions, it says that in this game, when one player is combative, the other player is better off giving in!

Finally, this is also a game where pretending to be crazy can work in your favour! Imagine that before starting the head-on collision race, one driver removes the steering wheel from his car. This person has effectively pre-committed to not swerving. Knowing this, the other driver might just swerve. Another way to signal you might be crazy, is to guzzle down half a bottle of Johnny Walker's finest in front of the other driver. This will signal that you are drunk and Dutch courage might prompt you to do crazy things and therefore it is best to back out.

A moment's reflection should also tell you, that you need not be the only one who can pretend to be crazy. Game theory always tells us to assume that the other player is just as smart as you are. Now, you have a dilemma—do you assume that the other player is really crazy or are they simply pretending? Of course, the other player also faces the same dilemma regarding you.

Bottom line: The one who can convince the other person that they are crazy will win this game! And therefore, the moral of this story is that *sometimes it pays to be crazy*.

Appendix 2: A Combination of Chicken and Bullying

The matrix below shows a game that combines Chicken with bullying. Let us denote Player 2 as the one who likes to bully. Each player has two strategies: to cooperate with the other player (C) or bully them (B). When there is no bullying (C, C), Player 1 still gets a little more since he escapes bullying. This game is different from Chicken since the bottom-left and top-right cells do not lead to symmetric payoffs. When Player 1 bullies and Player 2 cooperates (B, C), they get 3 and 0, respectively. In (C, B) the bully still gets 3, but Player 1 also gets a little something, i.e., 1, because they give in to the bullying and are not beaten up. It is like when the local *gunda*, thug, comes asking for his weekly *hafta*, and you hand over the extortion money, you do not get beaten up and live to tell the tale. On the other hand, if Player 1 decides to stand up to Player 2 (the gunda), player 1 gets beaten up and gets nothing while the bully gets 2 because they had to fight and win.

		Player 2	
		C	B
Player 1	C	2, 1	1, 3
	B	3, 0	0, 2

In this game, the bully is always better off bullying (compare his payoff from column B to column C: 3 is better than 1 and 2 is better than 0). Thus, B is what game theorists call a '*dominant strategy*': regardless of what the other player chooses, a dominant strategy is always better for you. So if you happen to have a dominant strategy, you should always play it.[1] Since Player 2 will always play B, we do not need to concern ourselves with what will happen in the column C. Player 1 compares only what happens under the outcomes (C, B) and (B, B). Clearly, they are better off choosing C (since 1 is better than 0). This also tells us why the weak are better off submitting to the alpha male in pack animals—they escape bullying and get protected!

If you have enjoyed reading *Calvin and Hobbes*, you will immediately realize that this is also the tale of Calvin and the quintessential school bully Moe! Moe always bullies Calvin: he either threatens to beat him up or actually carries out his threat. Back at home, Calvin makes grand plans about how to get back at Moe and evade the situation, but once he is in school, his courage generally deserts him and he hands over his lunch money to Moe, or he gets beaten up and regrets his courage.

---

[1] Note that the original Game of Chicken does not have a dominant strategy for either player. This game has a dominant strategy only for Player 2—the bully. Some games like the Prisoner's Dilemma have a dominant strategy for both players.

And now for a little quiz: The Nash equilibrium of this game is _____ .

(i)   C, C
(ii)   C, B
(iii)   B, C
(iv)   B, B

The First Piece of Cake . . .

A few weeks ago, my daughter's best friend was at our house. Over time, it had become customary to offer the two girls something small but sweet, usually midway through their play date. So, I went up to them and held out two *different* pieces of chocolate in my hand. To my consternation, instead of letting her friend choose first, my daughter grabbed a piece. You can predict what happened later that evening after her friend had left. We had a talk! I told her pointedly that when we have a guest, she has to let them choose first. Pat came my daughter's response, 'I know that my friend likes the other chocolate [i.e., not the one she took]. So does it matter that I took it first? We both got the chocolates we wanted!'

That got me thinking—why do we have to offer the guest the first choice? There are at least two scenarios that I can think of where this is not necessary. First, consider my daughter's example: the guest and host each like different things, and both know what the other wants. Then does it matter who goes first? Second, if food is in limited supply, survival instinct suggests that you should grab the food first, i.e., from an evolutionary perspective it is completely justified. In fact, by forcing her to go second, I am forcing my daughter to unlearn her survival instinct! A variant of this argument says that whoever is hungrier, should go first. This would generate the maximum utility or satisfaction for society from the first slice of cake. Then the second hungriest person would generate the second highest level of satisfaction and so on. Clearly, this is the efficient solution, i.e., the outcome that maximizes society's benefits and utility.

You First

So where did this '*pehle aap*' business come from? Here are some common answers—you let the guest go first because it is polite to do so (people want to seem selfless) or you are adhering to a cultural or spiritual practice. We believe in '*Aathi devo bhava*' or that a guest is akin to god and so on. But this still begs the question *why*?

I want to tackle this in two different ways—first, I will provide purely selfish reasons (those which do not require politeness or altruistic feelings towards others) for why we may want to offer the first piece to our guest. Second, I will examine it from a historical perspective. This latter analysis will be aimed at illustrating why such a practice might be enshrined in culture or religion.

The question we need to examine is why do we insist that the guest go before us? Among friends, as my daughter argued, it is not necessary to follow such protocol.[1] However, with an actual guest (a person with whom we lack familiarity), there are a number of economic reasons why we fuss over them and want them to go first. By insisting that they partake before you, you are making it clear that *you made the first offering*. Moreover, by letting the guest take

---

[1] While her response may have been right from an evolutionary perspective and following protocol may not have been necessary since she was dealing with a friend, as a parent, I still think 'the talk' was necessary since I want her to learn etiquette. In other words, at times we may do things that we think are irrational because we want to fit in with some sort of behaviour norm or follow etiquette!

the first piece of cake, you make them feel special. Both of these are wonderful things to do if you want to start a new relationship with your guest. Think of a first date—regardless of who arranged it (assuming you are interested), you make every attempt to create a favourable impression. Historically, another selfish reason could be, in an era when food was relatively scarce, offering food to the guest first was possibly to show that you can afford to forgo the food, suggesting thereby that you are strong and therefore a worthy friend and ally.[2] A final selfish reason may be 'warm glow'. This is an idea put forth by economist Jim Andreoni who argues that we derive pleasure or get a warm glow inside from doing our part to help others or being nice to them. This is why selfish people, for instance, may contribute to charity or offer the first piece of cake to others.

Next, let us examine why the practice of offering the first piece to the guest might become a part of cultural or religious practice. Historically, when food was not as abundant as it is now, the idea of offering the limited amount of food to the other person first was a way to signal that they were very important to you. Note that this required you to resist the temptation of consuming the limited food (or the bigger piece of cake) yourself. Religion often plays a big role in helping fight such

---

[2] All of these are reminiscent of a practice studied extensively by anthropologists and economists called 'gift-giving'. Kings in ancient India often ostensibly gave away large amounts of gifts—this was not just *daan* for *punya*, donations to earn karmic credit, it was also to demonstrate their wealth to others. A similar practice called 'potlach' was practised by Native American tribes in the north-west Pacific coast that consisted of giving away all their possessions. The Kularing practice in Papua and New Guinea was a similar idea where people undertook dangerous sea voyages to exchange what would be considered trifles.

temptation. By putting the guest on the same pedestal as god, it functions like a *commitment device*. What do you do if you have a hard time getting up in the morning? You set an alarm. What do you do if you want your soldiers to fight really hard in a battle? Burn the bridge after crossing it so that there is no going back—it is now a fight to the finish! Those familiar with Asterix comics will probably remember Julius Caesar repeatedly saying '*Alea jacta est*', meaning the die is cast which expresses the same idea of no turning back.[3] Moreover, in India, the deal is sweetened by saying that if you treat your guest well, you earn punya, thus improving your chances of going to heaven. And so religion tells us to offer the first piece of cake to the guest!

Why might culture require that we make our guests feel special? Travel was not easy in the ancient times. However, travel was necessary for trade, and trade is what brought us new ideas and products we did not have.[4] Given the vulnerability of travellers, to encourage travel, it was necessary to offer generous hospitality and treat guests very well. This led to a culture of hospitality, embodying the 'pehle aap' principle. In fact, some scholars argue that places with harsher travel conditions developed stronger cultures of generosity and hospitality. For instance, in the Middle East people go out of their way to be hospitable.[5]

---

[3] When Caesar's term as the governor ended, the Roman Senate asked him to disband his army and return to Rome. He was explicitly forbidden from crossing the river Rubicon. In January of 49 AD, Caesar did cross the Rubicon and is supposed to have muttered the phrase 'the die is cast'.

[4] Unfortunately, this movement of people and goods also brought new diseases like the plague or in modern times pandemics like Covid-19.

[5] Egypt is well known for this. If you meet someone who is in the middle of a meal, they will invite you to join them; if you want to buy

Multiple Guests

Up until now, we have been discussing a situation where there is one host and one guest. Suppose you decide to invite multiple (let us say, two or more) guests. Who should get the first piece of cake now? One simple solution to dealing with the issue is that you take charge as the host and you impose your rules: you determine the order in which the guests will eat. For instance, you could simply make the rule that older women will eat first and then everybody else. Another rule could be that those who arrived first will eat first.

Alternatively, you may choose not to enter into this mess at all. You simply offer the food to your guests and walk away— your job as a host is done (an excellent reason to organize a buffet party). Let the guests decide who will eat cake first. Common responses to this situation are: let them all eat together (which we rule out for the sake of argument) or let the oldest person or youngest person go first.[6] These latter choices can be put down to cultural norms, and it is also easy to see why. These two groups are more vulnerable than the other age groups. Economic efficiency, which we have already mentioned, can be

---

something from a friend, it will be suggested that you do not need to pay, and so on. Of course, you are expected to smile, and politely decline. In fact, this ceremonial behaviour even has a name—it is called 'a sailor's invitation'. Imagine two sailors on their individual boats in the middle of a large waterbody, each inviting the other to come on to their boat. Obviously, neither sailor can really leave their own boat and get on the other one. So it is not a real invitation, but it is a signal of politeness and generosity to others.

[6] Observe that instead of you telling them to do this, the guests may also impose such a rule on themselves.

very different from fairness and requires that we ask the guests to announce their intensity of hunger and let the hungriest person eat first. Alternatively, we can ask the person who has travelled the farthest to eat first simply because, like our ancient travellers, they might be the most in need of nourishment, or may have to travel back the farthest. What about fairness? If we are to be truly impartial, then we should randomly pick who goes first and who goes second, etc.[7]

Sometimes we may have to worry about a related problem of fairness—what if the first person eats the entire cake and leaves nothing for the second person? A lot of parents can provide you with an easy and impartial solution to this problem. Ask one child to cut the cake and ask the other child to pick the first piece! Thus, when there are only two people, the problem is easy to solve. But what if there are multiple guests? Then we simply ask every guest to write down how they want to cut the cake and tell them that we will pick one person's suggestion at random and cut the cake according to it. However, a different guest will be randomly chosen to select the first piece. As long as they all know this, we will get a fair division of the cake—unless, of course, someone is dieting!

---

[7] Observe that this is no longer just about cake. Suppose there exists a scarce resource for which there are multiple users: like who gets to board the bus first or who gets to use the university's high-powered computing resources first. If you control access to this resource, then you are like the host. You can make your own rule for how the resource will be allocated or you can let the users (the guests) make up the rules for allocating the resource. And once again it is easy to see that there may be a difference between the efficient and fair way to allocate the cake or the shared resource.

Multiple Hosts

Incidentally, what if there are multiple guests and multiple (let us say, two or more) hosts. Once the guests have eaten, in what order should the hosts eat? While we can use any of the mechanisms discussed above, typically, joint hosts should not have the need to impress each other, and therefore, the most commonly observed outcome is that they eat together. This may also help us understand the practice of eating from the same plate in Islamic cultures. Since everyone belongs to the umma, or the community, no one is unique, there is no hierarchy or the need to impress anyone. Therefore, nobody needs to go first. So everyone can eat at the same time—thus like one big happy family, they all sit down to eat together from one big communal plate!

The Last Piece of Cake . . .

At this point it almost seems unfair to ignore the fate of the proverbial last piece of cake or pizza or your favourite food that comes in discrete pieces.[1] All of us at some point or the other have been at a gathering where the last piece of food visibly remains on the table—no one *seems* to want it. Everyone leaves it alone for the others and if you are at a restaurant, everyone will pass the thing along to the next person at the table saying, 'This one is yours, I am already full.' Sometimes this tamasha does not end and the last piece remains on the table. At other times, someone finally gives in to temptation and with words like, 'Okay, if you insist' or 'Let's not waste food' grabs that last piece, making it seem like they have done everyone else a favour. The question is—why all this song and dance with the last piece?

But let me first rule out places and situations where this tamasha does not happen—most certainly, the last piece will not be left alone on the table under chronic food shortage or in places like Thailand where it is believed that the person who

---

[1] Unlike the typical economics problem, this story works better for the discrete case. The 'continuity argument' is a bit more complicated here—trying to tell the tale of the last piece of halwa or the last bit of payasam just does not have the same ring to it as the case of the last rasgulla.

eats the last piece of food at a meal will be lucky.[2] It also does not happen within the family—if anything, there might even be a fight for that last piece. It will never happen among hostel mates—imagine sitting in your hostel room with a bunch of friends and drinking Old Monk—or whatever else people drink in hostels these days—and everyone passing up on that last chicken wing (Yahoo News had this story about a man in Houston, Texas, who actually stabbed the friend that ate the last piece of chicken)!

Just like the story of the first piece of cake, basically, this story also needs a level of unfamiliarity among the participants—an event like an office party where a significant number of people are mere acquaintances and the edible item in question is visible to all.[3] Then one explanation is that everyone wants to impress the others by demonstrating that they have great self-control. The motivation for leaving the last piece untouched could be similar to why no one wants to take the first piece—just to make a good impression.[4] Another possibility is that everyone refrains from taking the last

---

[2] Several people have also informed me that in northern India, it is believed that having the last piece will guarantee you a handsome husband or a beautiful wife, as the case may be. I am not sure what happens when the people involved are already married—does it improve the appearance of their spouses?

[3] It is also possible that there are events where some guests are family and the others, family or not, are acquaintances—like at the birthday party of your future wife's grandmother that includes her entire extended family! In this situation, you may be one of the few people trying to impress everyone else.

[4] Another example of such behaviour in parties is the fact that often everyone is simply waiting for someone to be the first to hit the food and start eating.

piece simply because they do not want to be perceived as the greedy person who ate the last piece: everyone wishes to appear selfless! Hence, this piece is sometimes referred to as the 'decency piece' or the 'politeness piece'. In German there is even a term for the last piece: '*das Anstandsstück*'.[5] Most cultures have something similar where the last piece is left for the guests. The people of the state of Minnesota in the US are obsessive about this; there is even a Facebook page called 'Cursed Last Bites of Minnesota', with pictures of little bits of food left on the plate. Thus, one could argue that not going for the last piece is about showing that you are not greedy and care about others, you are altruistic and believe in 'sharing is caring'.[6] In fact, one suggestion to deal with the last piece is to take a small chunk from it and still leave something on the plate.

More to It than Meets the Eye

However, I feel that there is more to this story of visibly leaving the last piece on the plate. If I simply wanted to impress the others about my superior character, why not simply announce that I do not want the last piece? We could all make this announcement to establish our superior characters and be done. Except that most likely this is really an option only in a small cosy setting with a few people and not in large groups. Alternatively, we could all

---

[5]   The alternative word *Höflichkeitsgeste* may sometimes be used instead, though my German friends inform me that this really means 'gesture of politeness' and can be used more broadly, like when someone holds the door open for the next person.
[6]   This is a phrase that kids all across the US already learn in kindergarten. Perhaps it is no surprise therefore that no one wants to take that last piece of cake.

throw away the last piece or store it in the refrigerator. But we don't do that—and for good reason. You could simply ask why would anyone, since they are mere acquaintances, believe my announcement regarding my good character? More importantly, as long as the gathering can see that last piece, you all already know that I am selfless—I do not even need to declare my altruistic nature anymore. This is what really matters for my argument. The proof of the pudding, in this instance, is really not in the eating!

Actually, since we can all see that last piece of cake, we can say more. We can now make the following statements:

- *you know that* I am selfless, and
- *I know that* you know that I am selfless.

With a little more introspection, I can even say that

- *you know that* I know that you know that I am selfless,

and so on . . . ad infinitum.

In fact, we can say even more. Because that piece of cake is still there on the table,[7]

- *I know that* you are selfless, and
- *you know that* I know that you are selfless, and

so on . . . ad infinitum.

In fact, *we all know* that we all know that we all know . . . ad infinitum that we are selfless! In other words, this practice of

---

[7] In fact, the solution suggested for solving the last-piece problem takes this into account. The solution is to always take half of the remaining piece. If everyone keeps doing this, then there is always something left for the table—possibly crumbs at the very end, and it is not possible to assign blame to anyone for taking the last piece.

leaving the last piece of cake has created 'meta knowledge' about the fact or the message that we are an altruistic community.

Tip of the Iceberg

This convention associated with the last piece that I will call a 'public ritual' is not an isolated event—look around you and you will find plenty of religious and non-religious practices that serve the purpose of creating awareness or knowledge of an idea. In a fascinating book titled *Rational Rituals*, political science professor, Michael Chwe, of UCLA explains how public rituals serve to create knowledge of other peoples' knowledge, knowledge about other people's knowledge of other peoples' knowledge, and so on. To quote him, 'A public ritual is not just about the transmission of meaning from a central source to each member of an audience; it is also about letting audience members know what other audience members know.'

Prof. Chwe's book is replete with examples of public rituals to explain his idea. Take group dancing, for instance: it conveys meaning to the group through movement. Everyone knows that everyone else is paying attention; otherwise the movement will lose its harmony. He also argues that circular public structures for meetings, like a kiva,[8] or like the one in the movie *On the Waterfront*, help create this kind of meta knowledge by maximizing the possibility of eye contact among the participants. Instead of going into details of all the possible

---

[8] A kiva is circular structure associated with the Pueblo Indians who can be found in the south-western part of the United States. It was primarily used for religious rituals and political meetings.

examples, let me explain the key idea on which his book is based: *Common Knowledge.*[9]

Common Knowledge

I learned my game theory when it was customary to start any discussion on common knowledge (or any concept in game theory, for that matter) with a story. A story by the mathematician J.E. Littlewood is usually recounted in the context of common knowledge. It goes as follows: 'Three ladies A, B and C in a railway carriage have dirty faces and are all laughing. It suddenly flashes on A: why doesn't B realize that C is laughing at her?— Heavens! I must be laughable.'

If you are puzzling about how A came to this conclusion that she must be the one being laughed at, consider a more explicit Indian variation of the same story. Imagine *a group of people* are having *pau bhaji* on the beach. At the end of the meal, some of

---

[9]   I draw heavily on the *Stanford Encyclopedia of Philosophy* to explain the notion of common knowledge. The notion is truly interdisciplinary— it interests philosophers, economists, game theorists and computer scientists and falls in a field of study called epistemology, or the study of knowledge. Although the mathematician Littlewood (friend of G.H. Hardy, Ramanujan's host in Cambridge) discussed some examples pertaining to common knowledge, the Princeton philosopher David Lewis was the first to discuss the idea of common knowledge in his work *Convention*. It is believed that Lewis himself was influenced by Thomas Schelling's classic book *The Strategy of Conflict*. Robert Aumann (who shared the Nobel Prize for economics in 2005 with Schelling) was the first to provide a mathematical formalization of the notion of common knowledge in an interestingly titled paper called 'Agreeing to Disagree'.

these folks, say, k of them, have little bits of bhaji on their faces. Since no one can see their own face, none of these individuals knows whether he or she has a dirty face. At this point, the cook who made the pau bhaji returns with piping hot jalebis. Amused by what he sees, the cook rings a bell and makes the following (truthful) announcement: 'At least one of you has bhaji on your face. I will ring the bell repeatedly, till people with dirty faces have cleaned up. Then I will serve the jalebis.'

Surprise! Surprise! For the first k-1 rings, no one does anything. Then, at the k-th ring, everyone, i.e., all the k people with a dirty face suddenly reach for a napkin, and shortly afterwards, everyone is able to tuck into delicious jalebis.

So how did the people with dirty faces finally realize that their faces needed cleaning? To understand this, imagine that the Gaitonde family of three is having bhaji on the beach. Suppose only Mr Gaitonde ($k = 1$) has a messy face. Following the cook's announcement and the bell ring, he will realize immediately that he has a dirty face since he can see that everyone else's face is clean. Next, suppose both Mrs and Mr Gaitonde ($k = 2$) have a dirty face. After the first bell, Mrs Gaitonde knows that one other person, *Mr Gaitonde*, has a dirty face and Master Gaitonde does not, but does not yet know about herself. At the second bell ring, *Mrs Gaitonde* realizes that she must have a dirty face, since Master Gaitonde has a clean face and Mr Gaitonde has a dirty face. More importantly, she reasons that had *Mr Gaitonde* been the only one with a dirty face, *he* would have known this after the first ring, since he was able to observe Mrs Gaitonde and Master Gaitonde, and would have cleaned his face then. But he did not. Ergo, Mrs Gaitonde figures out that he must be able to see another person with a dirty face and since it was not Master Gaitonde, it must necessarily be her. A similar argument allows Mr Gaitonde to conclude that he has a dirty face at the second ring, and both pick up a napkin at that time. The general case including Master Gaitonde ($k = 3$), and beyond ($k \geq 3$) follows by induction and I will let the interested reader find the argument from the *Stanford Encyclopedia of Philosophy*

The 'paradox' here is that for $k > 1$, the cook's announcement informed everyone something that each already knew. Yet somehow the cook's announcement still provided everyone with useful information. How? By announcing a fact already known to everybody, the cook made this fact *common knowledge*, that is everyone now knew what everyone knew and so on, among these participants. Consequently, each of them was eventually able to deduce the condition of his/her own face after the bell had been rung for the appropriate number of times.

Uncommon Knowledge

Somehow the notion of common knowledge reminds me of a classic British whodunnit where a bunch of rich people are gathered together, possibly having cake and sherry while a body is found in the library. Then a cerebral armchair detective will discover the perpetrator of the crime through sophisticated reasoning. I guess this is because common knowledge requires us to make these multiple levels of *I know that you know that I know* . . . type of reasoning.

We do not usually think about common knowledge type reasoning, that is, engage in levels of reasoning, and yet it is a critical component of many things we do. Fundamentally, much of game theory relies on the fact that the structure of the game and the players' rationality is common knowledge. It brings to the fore our own beliefs and our beliefs about how others play and the role such beliefs play in shaping outcomes. This is illustrated beautifully by Professor Kaushik Basu in his recent book titled *The Republic of Beliefs*. At the risk of oversimplifying, among other things, he asks the following questions: What changes when something—that was earlier only a civic duty, for instance—is written down as a law? Why will people who were not following it till the day before suddenly act differently and start obeying the new law? One explanation that he offers for this is that once the law is written down, it becomes common knowledge. Now, suddenly, everyone, including those who have to follow it and those who have to enforce it, know about the law and know that the other party knows that they know about the law, and so on.

In fact I just want you to mull over my favourite lines from that book because I have not come across anything that explains the role beliefs play in our lives better: 'In truth, the most important ingredients of a republic, including its power and might, reside in nothing more than the beliefs and expectations of ordinary people going about their daily lives and quotidian chores. It is in this sense that we are all citizens of the republic of beliefs.'

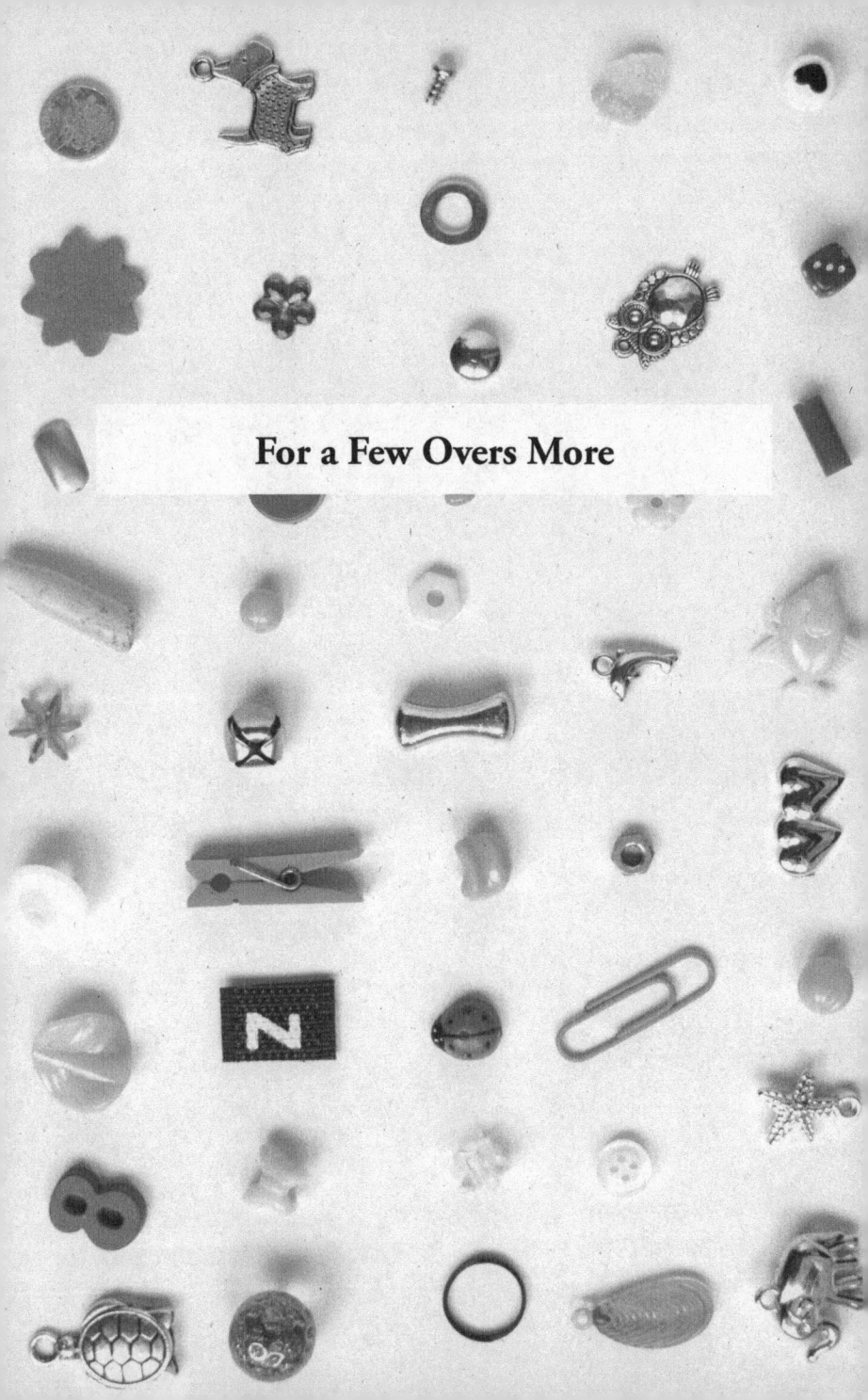

For a Few Overs More

This lunch conversation took place in Baton Rouge, Louisiana, several years ago between Dr Colin Cannonier, Dr Bibhudutta Panda and me.[1] We were arguing about whether the Twenty-Twenty (T20) format required a different style of play from that of the One Day International (ODI) matches. The question being debated was: Will it change a team's approach to the game? I had completely forgotten about this episode till July 2019, when, on my summer visit to India, I was passing through Kolkata and happened to read the *Telegraph*.[2] It was here that I read a piece about Dukes and Kookaburra—the two different types of balls used in most international cricket. The Kookaburra, as should be evident from the name, is made in

---

[1] Back then, Bibhu and Colin were both graduate students at Louisiana State University. Dr Panda now teaches at the University of Minnesota-Morris and Dr Cannonier at Belmont University. Moreover, in his even more youthful days, Colin had been the captain for both St Kitts and the Leeward Islands and was a much more serious cricketer than the two Indians.

[2] I have many fond memories of this newspaper. Growing up in Rourkela, the *Telegraph* provided a welcome change from the sombre *Statesman*. But what I really enjoyed reading in the *Telegraph* was the legendary Neil O'Brien's weekend quiz column with its questions and reports about quizzing at the Dalhousie Institute in Kolkata.

Australia.[3] The white Kookaburra ball is used in all T20 and ODI matches. While England and the West Indies use the England-made Dukes balls for Test matches, the other Test-playing countries use the red Kookaburra balls. We in India have our own low-cost brand for Test matches—Meerut-based Sanspareils Greenlands, also known as SG, provides hand-made crickets balls that are used in Test matches and Ranji Trophy matches in India.

The same article also informed me that the proud owner of Dukes was an Indian businessman called Dilip Jajodia. Mr Jajodia went on to explain that his company's product with hand-stitched seams was different from the machine-stitched Kookaburra balls. He explained that the machine-stitched ball has two rows of stitches, while the six rows of stitches on the hand-stitched ball allow it to retain its shape even after sixty overs. He said, 'The Dukes ball is crafted to deteriorate slowly over eighty overs. Whereas the seam on a machine-stitched ball tends to go flat after being whacked around for sixty overs . . .' Therefore, once again—how much do a few more overs matter? Now, I am going to tell you how Bibhu, Colin and I settled our debate.

Our solution was simple—exploit the information that is already out there. Examine how the winning strategy in a T20 game compares to the winning strategy in an ODI game to see if the additional thirty overs do make a difference. Popular opinion suggests that T20 is formulaic, with little scope to implement any cricketing strategy. Its critics say that T20 has reduced the traditional 'bat versus ball' contest to an attacking 'six-hitting' batting versus a defensive 'in-swinging yorker' bowling contest.

---

[3] The kookaburra or, more generally, the laughing kookaburra, is a kingfisher native to Australia and like many unusual things found Down Under, rarely eats fish.

The Data Set

We collected data for both ODI and T20 matches that took place during 2008 and 2009 from publicly available sources like ESPN's Cricinfo. Our data consisted of innings-specific aggregate information on a number of variables for each team. For T20, we also separately considered twenty-over international (T20I) matches (with countries as teams) and the Indian Premier League (IPL) where clubs with players from different countries in the same team compete. The logic for using international games was simple: players in international matches have years of international and domestic cricketing experience and are trained by long-term strategists and coaches. To obtain insights about how the optimal strategy changed once we changed the format, it was necessary to focus on games involving such players. Our choice of a club-level league was guided by the fact that the IPL has emerged as the most successful T20 league. Hence, it would be interesting to see how the optimal strategy changed once we moved from international cricket to league cricket. Our data set covered 276 ODIs played by eighteen teams during 2008–09. This period also included 118 IPL games involving eight teams and a total of seventy-seven T20I matches between sixteen teams in 2008 and twelve teams in 2009. We excluded information on seventeen ODI, four T20I and four IPL matches that were either abandoned or tied.

Our Methodology

We used a 'production function' approach that is common in the analysis of cricket by economists and statisticians. This approach considers the outcome of the game to be a function of batting, bowling, fielding and other relevant 'inputs' and, thus, enables us to determine the ideal winning strategy. At the aggregate or team level, these inputs can be measured in different ways, and to capture the intent of a team, we divide them into two categories: attacking and defensive.[4] Fielding is ascribed solely to the defensive category. Of course, these input measures are also affected by other observable and unobservable factors. Examples of observable factors for cricket are toss outcomes, home-team bias and weather conditions and can be included in the data set. Examples of unobservable factors include player ability and form, captaincy skills, coaching skills and team management skills. In the production function approach, when available, these factors are controlled for thorough statistical analysis.[5]

Next, we divided the batting and bowling inputs into two categories based on attacking and defensive intents. The batting variables were *runs scored through boundaries* (fours and sixes) as a per cent of total runs scored and *non-boundary runs* (excluding extras) as a per cent of total runs scored. The former may be thought of as an 'attacking' batting measure while the latter as a 'defensive' batting measure. The set of bowling variables comprised the following: *opposition wickets*

---

[4] Coaches make decisions and choose strategies for the team while also coaching individual players on what to do. This quantitative analysis of cricket uses data at the team level.

[5] It might be argued that a team's selection of batting or bowling approaches may be conditional on the choices made by the rival team. However, at the time of making its choice, a team may not be fully aware of the other team's choice. Hence, we identify the optimal combination of input measures independent of the opposing team's choices, except for the obviously known ones like team composition.

taken per over expressed as a per cent of overs and *the number of runs allowed through boundaries* (fours and sixes) as a per cent of total runs scored. Clearly, the first measure reflects attacking bowling intent while the second expresses a defensive bowling intent. Our fielding variable was defined as the *number of wickets attributable to fielding* (catches, stumpings and run-outs) as a proportion of the total wickets taken. Other independent variables included ones capturing whether a team played at home, whether a team won the toss and whether a team batted first.

We found that there are no significant differences in these measures (strictly speaking, in their means) between ODI and T20 matches or between the IPL and T20I matches. As popular opinion suggests, attacking batting plays a more important role in T20. Non-boundary runs, on the other hand, are more important in ODIs. Similarly, we find that contrary to popular opinion, T20 is not all about batting. We find that IPL is certainly the more aggressive format when it comes to batting, while attacking bowling is more important in T20I. It turns out that defensive bowling matters more in the IPL format while attacking bowling is important in the T20I format.

The average value for the fielding variable is significantly higher for T20 in comparison to ODIs. Similarly, the fielding variable has a higher mean in IPL than T20I. This raises an important statistical issue and requires us to be cautious when making inferences: Is the fielding performance higher in the formats where the stakes are higher or is this due to the fact that the faster rate of run accumulation creates more chances for the fielders in T20? We now look for insights beyond these simple averages by using regression analysis.

Optimal Input Combination

The insights presented below are neither specific to a team nor are they in response to a specific team's choices; they identify winning combinations of batting and bowling inputs for a team based on the format of the game. Assuming that the above 'inputs' determine the outcome at least at the aggregate level, we use econometric techniques—a conditional logistical regression—to rank the different measures of batting and bowling in terms of their impact on winning. A logistical regression predicts the probability of the occurrence of an event (in this case, winning) by fitting data (the relevant inputs) to what is called a logistic function. The conditional part takes the uniqueness of each game into account. We also test the validity of our results by using results from part of our sample to predict outcomes for the rest of the sample.

Attacking batting and bowling intents clearly emerge as the optimal combination for a team in both ODIs and T20I. In fact, defensive batting actually lowers the probability of winning both at the international and league levels.[6] However, the optimal combination for IPL turns out to be attacking batting and defensive bowling. Interestingly, for IPL, attacking batting leads to a greater increase in the probability of winning compared to the two international formats. Also, in contrast to ODIs and T20I, in IPL matches, a team that adopts attacking

---

[6] Of course, the game is in constant evolution. One way to understand these results is that with the preparation of more 'sporting' or balanced wickets in recent years, bowlers are playing a greater role in the outcomes of T20 matches. At the same time, the less docile pitches have forced batsmen to become more technically adept (or at least have tighter defences) but still maintain the attacking mindset.

bowling has a higher probability of losing. One possible explanation for these differences in results is that both ODIs and T20I involve national teams where players have years of international and domestic cricketing experience. Moreover, the teams are developed through long-term training by professional coaches and tips from think tanks and managers, and they end up spending a lot of time playing with each other. With such skilled batsmen and bowlers at their disposal and the opportunity to practise together for long periods of time, such teams have the necessary resources to adopt attacking batting and bowling measures. For teams in the IPL, on the other hand, it is more a motley crew of international and domestic players who do not engage in long practice sessions together. It could be argued that they have the same skill set, but lack synergies that can be found in a national team playing either of the two formats. Moreover, given the entertainment aspect, IPL certainly places a premium on run accumulation. Consequently, an IPL team might focus on strengthening its batting line-up in the recruiting process. Thus, one possibility might be that IPL teams lack the skill set and resources to pursue attacking bowling, and hence focus on limiting the opposition to a relatively lower total to maximise their winning probability.

Fielding and Other Inputs

The fielding variable does not have any significant impact on winning for any of the three types of games considered. This may be due to the fact that the fielding variable is only based on the wickets from fielding and does not account for its role in restricting runs. Unfortunately, the construction of a fielding variable that takes its dual role into account requires a ball-by-ball analysis of each match rather than aggregate match-level information. We find that winning the toss has no effect on the outcome of the game in any of the three formats. However, unlike ODIs and T20I, there is a significant home-team advantage in IPL.

Thus, it seems that there is not really much of a difference between ODI and T20 games, i.e., while twenty additional overs can affect the Kookaburra and the Dukes ball differently, the thirty overs make no difference to the winning strategy for these two cricketing formats.

Endgame Speculation

Cricket has undergone dramatic changes in the last fifty years. It's no longer the gentleman's game, played in the lush green countryside of England in five days; cricket today is quite a different cup of tea. The transition first happened with the fifty-over version in the early 1970s. In 2003, the even-shorter format, consisting of twenty-over innings and dubbed the T20, was introduced. Its most popular avatar is the IPL, which combines the excitement of limited-overs cricket—involving domestic as well as international players—and celebrity glamour into a single evening of entertainment. Right now, pink balls have already made their debut, and day-night Test matches are on the horizon.

What do we already know about the different formats? Well, most fans probably enjoy the one-evening T20 fanfare with plenty of action and a result at the end of the day. Players, too, possibly find the shorter version less stressful, and so can pack more into their schedules. On top of it, IPL is more lucrative as well. Therefore, given the popularity and significant monetary benefits that come with the game's shortest format, players are more likely to shift allegiance to this format. Such a transition becomes all the more feasible, since our analysis reveals that at the team level, there is no unique skill set required to excel in the T20 format (with the exception that the optimal bowling choice differs for league matches).[7]

The success of T20 does pose some challenges for the future of the game itself. League cricket itself has little interest in developing cricketing skills as players are pooled together only for a few weeks in return for large sums of money and there is even lesser incentive to nurture budding talent. The easiest way to counter this is for the cricketing nations to have specialized teams for the different formats. In fact, we are already seeing this: in general, there are different national squads for Test cricket and T20 with somewhat dissimilar squads for the two shorter formats. The growing popularity of T20 is creating pressure on national boards to accommodate more T20 matches in both their domestic and international calendars. Inspired by the success of IPL, many national boards are setting up domestic T20 leagues that will further crowd out other formats.

---

[7] A 2013 Federation of International Cricketers' Associations survey noted that 40 per cent of the respondents indicated a preference to play in the IPL even over their country. Additionally, 32 per cent of the respondents reported a willingness to retire prematurely, to keep playing unconditionally in these lucrative leagues.

Yet there will always be purists and lovers of the fine game of cricket in its pristine form.[8] It means Test cricket will remain, even though it may have to re-invent itself. As the erudite Rahul Dravid speculated, at some point the ODIs might feel the squeeze. While this is possible, since the majority of the ICC's revenues are currently derived from ODI matches, this format's decline in importance will certainly not be immediate. And someday when the three of us meet again for lunch, we will brood over this once more.

---

[8] Colin himself is one such person. My friend from childhood days, Arnab Roy, who lives and works in Bengaluru, is another such person. Interestingly, unlike Colin, Arnab was critical of our study published in the *Journal of Sports Economics*. I will not be surprised if this piece does divide the readers—my response simply is, different strokes for different folks.

Are More Choices Really Better?

W̲e live in a world obsessed with choices. Walk into a store to buy a pair of trousers or kurtis and you will be confronted by a wide array of colours, fabrics, styles and whatever other distinguishing feature that clothing designers can think of. The same goes for food. I still fondly remember sneaking up to my grand-aunt's pickle vats on summer afternoons when it was siesta hour for the elders (and the pleasure of getting to them without her knowledge). Today, you walk into any reasonable-sized grocery store and you will find all the pickles that my grand-aunt used to make, plus ones from every state in India, creating a serious dilemma for the buyer.

The Tyranny of Choice

I also remember, but not with equal fondness, my first visit to a Subway. It was August 1994 and I had just arrived in the US for graduate school. A friend who had already been there for a few years decided to take me to Subway for lunch. The number of decisions I had to make to buy a simple sandwich was mind-boggling—I almost felt like skipping lunch! Like many novices, in frustration, I even suggested to the server that he could put in whatever *he* liked. The server would not budge—it was my sandwich, therefore, I had to choose! For most of us who went to the US after growing up in pre-liberalization India, simple acts like ordering a sandwich or choosing a laundry detergent were incredibly difficult decisions in the US.

Things were even worse for students who came from Eastern Europe and the former Soviet republics. Growing up in economies that faced a perennial shortage of almost everything and a lack of variety, they were so bewildered by this vast array of choices that they often deferred purchasing things. Needless to say, for all of us foreign students who did not come from economies with a large number of choices, the weekly grocery trip took up an incredible chunk of time.

There was one criteria that worked for all of us poor graduate students: when all else failed, buy the *cheapest thing*, whether it was the laundry detergent or the milk gallon.[1] Thankfully, over time, your brain learns to adapt and soon, like our American friends, we were able to make these decisions without feeling oppressed by the number of choices. It was a good thing that I was already trained in the art of making choices before the advent of artisanal coffee promoted by Starbucks and its variants—imagine how painful it would be if buying a cup of coffee felt like a chore?

Why Do We Think More Choices Are Better?

Economists argue more choices are better simply because of the mathematical truism that choosing from an unconstrained choice set can never be worse than choosing from a constrained

---

[1] This is a perfect example of what scholars studying decision theory would call a *heuristic*: any approach to solving a problem that employs a practical method that may not be optimal, but instead is quick and sufficient for achieving an immediate and acceptable goal.

set. This mathematical truism simply says that pick your three favourite ice-cream flavours from the thirty-one flavours that Baskin Robbins offers. Suppose Baskin Robbins decides to discontinue eleven of those and you have to pick your favourites from out of the twenty available flavours. Clearly, you cannot be worse off in the first scenario, which offered thirty-one flavours. Therefore, more choices are better—unless of course, *it is costly to choose*. And here we are not referring to monetary cost, but whether the act of choosing itself is costly in terms of time and effort for your brain. If this turns out to be true, more choices may not be a very good idea!

Designing an Economic Experiment

Psychologists have been studying the consequences of '*choice overload*' for quite a while. Popular books written by psychologists such as Barry Schwatrz or Sheena Iyengar provide an excellent introduction to the concept of choice overload. When faced with more choices/options, people often do not choose at all, they say. Alternatively, they are not happy with their choice, i.e., the dish that the person at the next table has ordered looks better, and so on. However, imagine that you are interested in finding out whether people make the optimal/best choice for themselves (and not necessarily the one that makes them happiest) when faced with more choices. This is important if we are thinking about things like insurance plans or vitamin supplements, for example.

Some years ago, I along with a few friends decided to study this phenomenon of choice overload using an economic experiment. The goal of an economic experiment is to create a situation that captures the issue you wish to study in a lab, and pay people (not a flat amount as in a survey, but different amounts) according to their decisions. The payments should also be salient—in other words, if the experiment will take thirty minutes, the experimental participants should make at least as much as they could earn in that time by doing some other task. Thus, this lab experiment now mimics the economic situation that we want to study, has the appropriate amount of incentives in place, thereby ensuring that those who make good decisions will earn more and vice versa. Experiments in economics never use deception, because once you do this then the participants will no longer trust you and your attempt to study the economic phenomena at hand will be lost for good. Finally, an economic experiment generally poses the problem bereft of its context. This latter statement means that if I wish to study health insurance, then the experiment will mimic the task of choosing health insurance without any reference to health insurance at all. This is done to ensure that the prior knowledge and beliefs of the participants about health insurance do not interfere with their decisions—the only thing that should matter in the experiment are economic incentives!

Our Choice Experiment

In our experiment, every participant had to deal with eight different choice problems. First, participants in our experiment were shown six cards and the probabilities associated with these cards (Figure 1 that follows this chapter provides an example of a task in the experiment). You may consider these six cards to be diseases and the numbers under the 'Odds' column telling us how likely they will occur, i.e., the probability of the occurrence of each disease. Also on the screen were four different options or plans. The different plans provided protection or coverage against different diseases, and there was no plan that would protect against all six diseases.[2] This was the simplest choice problem in the set of eight problems. So all that was needed to be done was to find the plan that offered the maximum amount of protection or the highest chance of overall protection. How would you do that? As explained in Figure 1, it was simple: just add up the disease probabilities included under every offered plan, and find the plan that maximizes this number (has the highest expected value). Given the fixed disease probabilities, unlike food, in the psychology experiments, there is no subjective element in choosing a plan here—what was good for the goose was good for the gander. There is only one optimal or best plan for all the participants! What about the most difficult task in the experiment—it had ten cards or diseases and thirteen plans that covered these ten cards in different ways.

What we discovered was pretty striking—everyone made worse decisions when given more plans to choose from. Participants in the age group between eighteen to forty made the best decisions, giving credence to the popular saying that

---

[2] Note that there is no mention of disease or health. Moreover, different health insurance packages do cost different amounts of money. However, since we wanted to focus purely on whether having more plans mattered or not for finding the best plan, we assumed all plans cost the same amount—nothing! If we had introduced costs for these plans, it would have added another level of complexity and could have affected our results. Thus, we would not have found out whether their choices were affected by costs or because they had more choices. Basically the objective is to vary one thing at a time and study its impact on the task at hand.

it is, 'All downhill after forty!' Participants over sixty made dramatically worse decisions compared to everyone else. There were no gender differences, and there were no differences in the time used for making these decisions.[3] We were able to show that the results were not driven by differences among the groups in education among these people, nor was it the case that the elderly did poorly because they were not interested in making money in the experiment. After all, they had volunteered to participate in the experiment—we did not hold a gun to their heads and force them to choose a plan. Generally, if you make a conscious choice to play a game, you also do try to be the winner. However, just to be sure, we did conduct another experiment where we increased the payment for each successful task to ten times what we were paying originally. This had no impact on the performance of the elderly.

Finally, we decided to explore the possibility that the elderly or those over sixty were using a different criteria or heuristic than the other age groups. Recall, we have already talked about one heuristic that was common among graduate students: buy the cheapest product. Based on the data from our experiment, it seemed that the elderly were using a heuristic which is also called 'tallying'. This implies that you ignore the disease probability information given to you and assume that each of those six cards is equally likely (1/6) to occur. So if a plan includes four cards and

---

[3] Before you despair, we also found that having a college education helps in making better decisions. Though, as we found in another study, after the age of seventy-four, people simply make random choices. So the moral of the story is, take all the important decisions in your life before you hit that number.

another includes three cards, then the first one offers over protection of 4/6 and the second one 3/6, making the first one the preferred choice. Consequently, given seventy diseases or cards, it is possible that you prefer a plan that covers fifty obscure or low-probability diseases (50/70 in your head) over one that covers twenty (20/70) highly likely diseases.

The proof of the pudding is in the eating. Therefore, we lay a trap: we designed a new experiment containing a plan that covered more diseases than the best plan, but these diseases were less likely, just like in the example described above. Guess what—the elderly walked into our trap, while participants in the age group between eighteen and forty did not. This allowed us to conclude that compared to younger participants, the elderly were using a different and simple-minded reasoning process (aka heuristic) to solve the problem.

Shopping Tip

It is clear that by appropriately designing the choice sets they offer us, firms can take advantage of us. Most likely, they can exploit the elderly by offering them a larger set of health insurance or retirement plans. A follow-up experiment found out that when you are faced with a large array of choices, the best strategy is to set up a tournament between them. Suppose you have to choose between sixteen insurance plans—then divide them into four groups with four plans in each. Find the best plan in each of the four groups and then find the best plan from among these four winners. Keep that in mind the next time you are shopping and are having a hard time deciding which pair of shoes to buy.

Figure 1: Example of Sample Experimental Task

This is a screenshot of the simplest of the eight tasks in our experiment. Note that the participants are provided with detailed instructions about this process. I will briefly summarize what happens in the experiment. There are six possible cards numbered 1–6 which may be considered as possible diseases. The column numbered 'Odds' shows the probability of each card in percentage terms. Card 1 has a probability of 24 per cent, Card 2 of 8 per cent, and so on. Note that Card 4 has the highest probability of occurrence at 26 per cent. Given that the numbers in the 'Odds' column are probabilities, it can be checked that they add up to a 100. The participant can choose between four options—these are the columns labelled A,B,C,D. The check marks under each option show the cards they cover or include. Option A covers (or provides protection against) Cards 1, 3, 5 and 6. Option B covers Cards 2, 3, 5 and 6.

	Odds	Options			
		A select	B select	C select	D select
Card 1	24	✔		✔	✔
Card 2	8		✔		
Card 3	21	✔	✔	✔	
Card 4	26			✔	✔
Card 5	12	✔	✔		✔
Card 6	9	✔	✔		

Figure 1

In the experiment, participants have to choose a plan from the four shown on screen. Then the computer randomly picks one of the six cards (say, for example, Card 3). If the plan chosen by the participant includes the card then they get paid a reward. Otherwise, they earn 0. So in the experiment if you chose Plan A, B or C, you would get paid when Card 3 is chosen. Otherwise, you get 0. If Card 5 was picked randomly by the computer, then you would get paid if you had selected either Plan A, B or D, but not Plan C. If you had picked Plan C you would receive 0 when the computer picks Card 5.

Finding the Best Plan: If you pick Plan A, the odds that you will get paid are: 24+21+12+9 = 66 (got by summing the odds associated with the cards covered in the plan).

Doing the same calculation for all the other plans we have: For Plan B, the odds of being paid are: 8+21+12+9 = 50; for Plan C, the odds of being paid are: 24+21+26 = 71; and for Plan D, the odds of being paid are: 24+26+12 = 62. Note that Plan C offers the highest odds of getting paid or has the highest expected payoff. Therefore, this is the best plan for all participants. Unlike in the case of jams or jeans, there are no subjective elements here. Note that Plan C only covers three cards, while both Plans A and B cover four cards each. Yet Plan C covers the three cards with the highest odds and therefore is the best/optimal plan to choose for everyone.

P. G. Wodehouse, Futurist?

The name P.G. Wodehouse normally does not spring to mind when talking about futurists. Jules Verne, Arthur C. Clarke and Alvin Toffler certainly, but Pelham Grenville? Quite definitely not! Wodehouse is an author one associates with the affable Bertie Wooster and the inimitable dolichocephalic, fish-eating Jeeves. Others may conjure up visions of the muddle-headed Lord Emsworth and his magnificent beast—the Empress of Blandings.

But a die-hard Wodehouse fan will also tell you about Rupert Psmith and the other schoolboy stories the author penned. Though often ignored and usually somewhat hard to find, many unusual nuggets lurk in these innocuous tales. It is to one of these to which I want to draw attention. Titled 'An International Affair', it was published in a magazine called *The Captain* in 1905, and can be found in the Project Gutenberg free eBooks collection called *The Politeness of Princess and Other Stories*.

The title of the story suggests a John le Carre style thriller or a tale of espionage and intrigue but is far from it. The story is rather prescient—it reads like the classic tale of the neighbourhood mom-and-pop store facing the giant retailer. You could easily substitute the latter today with Walmart or Carrefour, or their Indian avatars like Big Bazaar or Reliance Fresh.

An Eerie Ring

The tale goes as follows: Oliver Ring, the American owner of Ring's Come-one Come-all Up-to-date Stores, happens to be passing through the lazy English countryside town of Wrykyn, home to the public school bearing the same name. The shop windows in Wrykyn resemble those in every other country town in England, having no initiative and none of that quality that would arrest a pedestrian's progress. In America, Mr Ring reflected, they did these things better, and this reflection arrested the capitalist pilgrims' progress. It dawned upon Mr Ring that this was the perfect place for setting up one of his megastores.

We are told that Mr Ring's Come-one Come-all Up-to-date Stores are well known all over the world, with offices in Broadway, New York, and others in Chicago, St Louis and St Paul within America. Overseas offices existed in London, Paris and Berlin—which in those days basically amounted to saying everywhere in the world. In Mr Wodehouse's words, 'The peculiar advantage of Ring's Stores is that you can get anything you happen to want there, from a motor to a macaroon, and rather cheaper than you could get it anywhere else.' If this does not sound like Walmart, I do not know what else would. Of course, Mr Wodehouse was writing in 1905, when one can only wonder where these multitudes of products were being produced. Not China, certainly.

In any case, once Mr Ring had taken his decision, an army of workers descended on the town, demolishing a bunch of tumbledown houses with a hitherto-unknown efficiency and building the new Come-one Come-all Up-to-date Store with incredible speed. Following that, the newspapers were flooded with the store's advertisements, and the Wrykyn School also receives its fair share of flyers. Local merchants, who till now had paid scant attention to competition and modern hustle and bustle, are woken from their slumber by this new phoenix of a store rising up right in their backyard. In this tale, the villain of the piece, Mr Ring's store, targets Cook's, the local chai shop and favourite haunt of the Wrykyn boys, by offering a heavily discounted afternoon tea.

David vs Goliath

The eponymous Cook's is run by Mr Cook, a former sergeant in a line regiment, his wife, Mrs Cook, who has the enviable ability to listen to five people simultaneously as well as supervise an invisible menial or menials. An atmosphere of gloom descends on Cook's as the schoolkids flock in droves to Come-one Come-all. Its owner feels 'haunted by the spectre of that hideous, new, glaring red-brick building down the street'. That is when a small group of loyal Davids decide to champion the cause of Cook's. In true British gentlemanly spirit, they first warn the newcomer to desist from destroying Cook's. In the story, Mr Wodehouse clearly casts his lot with the mom-and-pop store and in the end it's still Cook's cuppa tea. What strategy Mr Wodehouse allows his Davids to use to bring down Goliath, I leave the interested reader to find out.

Regardless of the outcome, this short story captures very well the ethos of the battle between today's *kirana* store and the big retailer, especially in urban India. The debate on retailing still continues. Right now, single-brand retailers are fine; a consensus still eludes multi-brand retail. And that seems hard, despite the Centre trying to reach out to the states and proposing conditions such as the retail chains having to source a third of its products in India. That will hopefully create new employment, even as Big Retail may well put the local stores out of business.

Even if a consensus may finally be reached, many battles like the one in Wodehouse's fictitious (or futuristic?) tale with their own Davids and Mr Rings may still be fought. In today's real world, of course.

Postscript: This is my very first piece of popular writing, published in *The Hindu BusinessLine*, on 12 June 2012. It is also why I had initially chosen to end the book with this piece—a sort of 'back to the beginning'; but then Covid-19 happened. As such, it is shorter than the other pieces. I have deliberately kept it almost identical to the original version, with a few stylistic changes, because I wanted the reader to read this piece in its original form.

In Freedom Begins Responsibilities

As I was finalizing the manuscript and adding the finishing touches, the entire world was in the midst of a once-in-a-lifetime crisis— the Covid-19 pandemic. Outbreaks like this offer many interesting insights into human behaviour and I had already been researching and writing on this topic. In fact, only recently in an essay comparing the London plague of 1665 to Covid-19, I had documented that in spite of advances in technology and the emergence of sociopolitical institutions like democratic governments, human behaviour is incredibly persistent, and you can identify similarities even though these epidemics were separated by 350 years. From this was born the idea of adding a chapter on the pandemic to this collection, and with the blessings and help of my editors at Penguin, I put together this new chapter just weeks before the book was sent to press. It is a collage of some my writings on the pandemic that are in the spirit of this book.

In the epigraph to *Responsibilities*, one of his collections of poems, William Butler Yeats noted that in dreams begin responsibilities. Given the surreal nature of our experiences in 2020, let's settle for the more mundane notion that responsibilities come with freedoms. Spring gave way to summer but the siege of the coronavirus SARS-CoV-2 continued, and people all around the world grew restless, hankering for normalcy. At the time of writing this chapter, only a handful of states in the US were in the 'Closed' category, while the rest fell into the 'Partially Open' category, a term open to varied interpretation, just like the many flavour options of Baskin Robbins ice cream. However, we are still in the midst of the pandemic, and even faraway places like Greenland and French Polynesia have reported positive Covid-19 cases.

Pandemics are outbreaks of infectious diseases that spread rapidly to large sections of humanity. They can last for considerable periods of time and quickly paralyse economic activity. They not only bring death, but also affect the living because of the uncertainty and fear they create. Prolonged economic deprivation is just one part; they affect overall well-being directly through a fall in living standards and the rise of sickness, and indirectly via acute social isolation. The Keynesian solution of increased government spending is simply not adequate here unless the health risks can be minimized, and fear of the disease dispelled. Consequently, pandemics like the current one tend to bring human behaviour into sharp focus by emphasizing the nature of constraints, and our inherent inability to predict future outcomes.

End of Lockdown

One of the biggest questions facing every country is not whether to end the lockdown or not, but when to open up. Let me try and sum up the different issues involved in this decision. We live in a time when medical science is the best it has ever been, and we like to claim that every life is precious, though in practice some lives count for more than others (suggesting we need to take into account what health resources we have and how much). Before we go any further, we have to recognize that the lockdown comes at a cost. My colleagues Shaowen Luo, Byron Tsang and Zichao Yang, for instance, have estimated that the stay-at-home orders for the period 19 March to 15 April 2020 cost the US economy $3521 per person. This alone suggests that in spite of all the misgivings, no country can stay closed forever.

The steps we take to tackle the heat in the summer provides an excellent analogy for the opening up of the economy. As the mercury shoots up and the sun bears down on us, we turn on the air conditioning (AC), the water cooler, fan or whatever other cooling device we have. This makes things better inside the house and provides us with relief from the heat. Similarly, closing down the economy by curbing human interaction has helped us check the infection. No one can claim credit for this exercise of flattening the curve because it is simply as mechanical an outcome as an AC cooling a room. In other words, if you switch off the AC, it will get hot again. Incidentally, outside the house it is still summer, and the coronavirus is still making its way around the country! The sooner we understand this, the better it will be for all of us. Therefore, as states relax stay-at-home orders, we as citizens need to be mindful. This freedom to venture out again and engage in economic activities marks the true beginning of our responsibilities: the burden of protecting our own lives and those we love is now on us.

One does not saunter out on a hot summer afternoon unless really necessary; but if needed, one takes precautions, like protective headgear, umbrella, adequate hydration, etc. Similarly, in the post-lockdown world, we need to follow all the steps necessary to keep ourselves safe: wear masks, wash hands, not go into crowded bars and shops. Of course, it is evident that staying indoors in the summer is a privilege that only the economically secure groups can afford, not those who rely on hourly work. So, too, is the case with this pandemic. Those who are economically the most vulnerable to the stay-at-home orders want it to end the soonest, but it is also these individuals (and the ones already fighting on the front line in the healthcare sector) who will therefore face the greatest exposure to the virus.

There is one more thing. In a pandemic, it is not sufficient that one person or one state follows the safety guidelines. An infectious disease creates a negative externality (as discussed earlier in the chapter titled 'Telegram'): if you get sick, you can pass it on to others. In order to prevent the loss of life, we need everyone to be heroes—people who want to save the lives of others. Thus, we need people who understand responsibility and are willing to follow safety measures even if it means that they have to sacrifice something.

But Do We Really Understand Responsibility

Let's compare two pandemics: Covid-19 and the 1665 plague outbreak in London as described by Daniel Defoe in his book *A Journal of the Plague Year*, published in 1722.[1] Interestingly, it seems that many aspects of human behaviour are quite robust and do not seem to have changed despite these events being separated by 350 years.

---

[1] A caveat is necessary here. Most scholars believe that while Defoe's account of the epidemic in London is fictional, it is still grounded in reality, albeit the connections might be somewhat tenuous at times. In fact, Anthony Burgess while writing the introduction to the Penguin edition of 1966 wrote: 'Defoe was our first great novelist because he was our first great journalist.'

The first officially confirmed deaths due to the plague in London were recorded in December 1664 and over the next few months thousands died. However, it was only effectively at the beginning of July 1665 that the authorities began taking actions like restricting movement to prevent the spread of the plague. Defoe notes, '. . . on which Act of Parliament the Lord Mayor and aldermen of the city of London founded the order they made at this time, and which took place the 1st of July 1665 . . .' Interestingly, these actions were initially limited to only parts of the city and not the entire city. Although the responses to Covid-19 have been remarkably different in different countries, a common denominator of policy response around the world has been denial in the early stages of the outbreak—just like the authorities in London during the plague outbreak took more than six months to respond. In 2020, a large number of countries imposed restrictions by dividing their country into zones based on the outbreak. Italy, for instance, had to order the lockdown of the entire nation when it became so imperative, but restrictions were initially imposed only on certain sections of the economy and in select parts of the country. In other words, this is how countries react and take responsibility in the initial stages of a pandemic.

What explains such striking similarities in the responses to these two pandemics that occurred 350 years apart? A simple economic explanation is that the primary objective of those in power, whether it is monarchy or democracy, has always been to stay in power. And, therefore, the actions of the government have been centred on ensuring re-election or their ability to continue in power. Since economic hardship makes re-election more difficult for the incumbent (as shown in a seminal paper by Yale economist Ray Fair published in 1978), governments, against the advice of health experts, kept businesses running until it was necessary to impose a lockdown.[2] Even when a lockdown was imposed, governments tried to put the blame on others rather than take the responsibility for their late and/or inadequate actions. Defoe notes that in the early stages, the plague in London was attributed to the Dutch and the authorities in London felt that its border controls would keep them safe.

With the beginning of the lockdown, both in the case of the plague of 1665 and Covid-19, one of the most common strategies for containment was contact tracing, monitoring and isolation. Given the technology available in 1665, these activities were carried out using human labour. Every parish appointed Examiners, whose duty was to identify the infected and order the constabulary to shut out the infected house completely. The job of ensuring that no one entered or exited the house of the infected during the plague in London was entrusted to individuals called Watchmen. Burial instructions were issued, and parties and events were prohibited to prevent the spread of the plague. For Covid-19, in India, contact tracing and monitoring is done largely through cell phone apps like Arogya Setu, though in some developing countries, human beings are frequently used as a substitute.[3] Again, the similarity in response is not surprising because it is the only solution once

---

[2] Adi Brender and Allan Drazen (2008), for instance, find that in developing countries economic growth is positively associated with the likelihood of re-election.

[3] In the London of 1665, online shopping or home delivery was not an option. So rich folks stayed at home and used their servants to interact with the outside world, like doing their shopping for them. Ironically, this was the channel through which the plague sometimes made it into the rich households and wiped out entire families.

authorities realize that they are dealing with an infectious disease. Implementation, however, is a different issue. Then, as now, many people tried to escape lockdowns by simply fleeing, or finding other ways to beat the system, like by bribing those who were supposed to monitor them or by using their connections to escape.

Opportunism

Pandemics are also a time of extreme opportunism— uncertainty and resource scarcity tend to exacerbate resource-hoarding behaviours. A very pointed instance of hoarding that Defoe describes in his book is when trying to escape the city to Lincolnshire, the author witnessed an acute shortage of horses for hire even though most people were not moving around the city. There are other instances where he talks about theft—for instance, of an unnecessary item like women's hats from an unguarded warehouse in London—as well as frequent descriptions of food shortages. Similar opportunism is witnessed in the current pandemic. The *New York Times* reported in one of its March 2020 articles how a seller in Florida was offering fifteen N95 face masks on Amazon for $3799, milk was being charged at $10 per gallon (which is at least twice the regular price) in a convenience store in Massachusetts and, of course, the most curious case where toilet-paper rolls were vanishing from stores and being offered at exorbitant prices.[4]

---

[4] Michael Levenson, 'Price Gouging Complaints Surge Amid Coronavirus Pandemic', *New York Times*, 27 March 2020, https://www.nytimes.com/2020/03/27/us/coronavirus-price-gouging-hand-sanitizer-masks-wipes.html.

Four and Twenty Rolls of Paper

But do you really need those twenty-four packets of toilet paper rolls while your neighbour has none? Shortage of necessities in modern times is typically man-made or artificial. Nobel Prize–winning economist Amartya Sen in his 1983 book on poverty and famines has argued that while it is commonly believed that famines are caused by decline in the availability of food, this is not the case in modern times. He carefully documented that the Great Bengal Famine of 1943, which killed between 2 million or 3 million people, is a classic example of starvation not always being related to the availability of supply.

The shortage of essentials like toilet paper, canned goods or onions (as happens regularly in India) is not because supply is limited, but simply because some people are buying up more than they need. In some cases, it is really due to hoarding or stocking up out of sheer panic without any regard for the needs of others. In other instances, it is to create artificial scarcity by hoarding a product with the goal of reselling at much higher prices to make a quick buck.

Fair Allocation

A common way to allocate things that are scarce is by rationing, such as a store limiting each customer to purchasing only a certain number for each product. Another interesting approach that economists or parents with multiple kids and the knowledge of game theory suggest for ensuring fairness is the 'divide and choose' rule—where one person is given the role of cutting the cake and the other person gets to choose the first piece. This will ensure that the person cutting the cake will split it equally.

Similarly, imagine every shopper is allowed to fill the cart with what they think are 'essentials' or 'bare necessities', to rephrase Baloo from *The Jungle Book*. Then each shopper is randomly assigned a cart filled with products selected by another shopper. And to keep things simple, assume that every cart has products totalling up to the same cost. It is important that in this random assignment a shopper never gets their own cart. This simple mechanism will ensure that everyone picks only what they think is essential; no one would overstock since they know they would never get their own cart. Certainly, this would prevent people from taking twenty-four packets of toilet-paper rolls. It is highly unlikely that the mechanism proposed here will actually ever be implemented in a store, but it captures the essence of this book—how simple economic principles pervade our life and can serve as a guide to behaviour. We are, after all, passing through an unprecedented time and we can only get through it if we work together. *We must think about the others in our community just as we want them to think about us.*

Coda

When I started working on this book, I did not intend for it to have a conclusion—my goal was simply to stop when I was done writing. However, my friend Michael Moehler, who is a philosopher, insisted that I absolutely needed a concluding chapter that listed the book's takeaways. What after all, he said, was the point of reading this book (or any, for that matter) if the reader does not get a summary of its essence at the end. At that point, I was in two minds—a part of me saw the sagacity behind his suggestion, but another part of me was still reluctant. A few days later, my wife finished reading the entire manuscript and asked me, 'Don't you have some sort of an epilogue?' There it was again—the demand for a concluding chapter, and I asked her the same question: Why was it necessary? My wife, whose wisdom regarding such matters I put a lot of faith in, simply stated that a conclusion is necessary to complete the manuscript. Readers expect one, and besides it is necessary to end on a strong note, she informed me in a very matter-of-fact manner. Although little tendrils of defiance kept swirling around in my head, at that point I decided that it was unwise to ignore the joint wisdom of your spouse and your philosopher friend.

In my mind, this book is about how economic ideas pervade our everyday lives. They are present in many little things like a piece of cake and sometimes in big ones too like the end of the era with the shutting down of telegram services. Yet, as far as takeaways go, most introductory economic textbooks provide an excellent and succinct list of what the key ideas in economics are. Harvard Professor N. Gregory Mankiw's *Principles of Economics* has a great introductory chapter that lists the 'Ten Principles of Economics'. There is certainly no point in my repeating those again. So, this is an attempt to organize my key ideas into that final piece suggested by two wise people without being repetitive.[1]

- *Incentives matter*: This is probably the most obvious one for economic behaviour. Performance bonuses and commissions exist simply to incentivize people to work harder. Remember what happened to the children of Hamelin when the Mayor failed to pay the promised amount. This is what drives the best products out and also why the guy from Rourkela is more likely to buy the premium ticket at Cuttack's Barabati Stadium. Non-monetary incentives can be just as important—people do care about awards like the Employee of the Month or that big corner office with large windows. Recognition amongst peers, the raison d'etre for any award, is very important (and often a cheap way) for incentivizing behaviour. More importantly, better incentives

---

[1] If you wish to stand in solidarity with my tendrils of defiance, please feel free to skip this coda.

might prevent employee turnover, cutting down the cost of having to train new recruits, i.e., efficiency wages are crucial. Incentives, however, also have unintended consequences and can lead to things like moral hazard. Providing someone with automobile insurance or seat belts may make them drive more—or more recklessly. And finally, as we know from the cobra effect, offering money for dead rats may lead to more live rats!

- **Heterogeneity matters**: People are not all the same, and whether this is a good or a bad thing depends on the context. We have different tastes in wine, whisky and mangoes. We have different skills—for instance, some of us are considerably better at teaching French or the fine art of sophistry than others. This is why we have all those varieties of masala oats and so many different types of résumés.[2] Since different people like different levels of comfort in their airplane or train seats, or like a professor and a student have a different value for time, it gives firms an opportunity to sell different products at different prices, thereby making higher profits. Just like firms, people also react to the heterogeneity around them and we learn and do things for each other. Sadly, it may also lead to unfortunate situations like my colleague from Cameroon who is increasingly paranoid about being stopped on the road by cops, or the fact that Muslims are increasingly finding it hard to rent an apartment in some places in India. Taste-based discrimination exists because people have different preferences while statistical discrimination arises

---

[2] I would also like to believe that this is the reason why we have so many different political parties in India, though I suspect dynastic politics has more to do with that.

because certain groups may be associated more frequently with certain types of outcomes. The heterogeneity of economic agents thus induces a separate cost-benefit calculus of its own that impacts economic activity in significant ways. Keeping this fact in mind helps, especially in matters like price discrimination.

- ***Complementarities matter***: The absence or presence of the savoury snack *mathri* can significantly impact the experience of your next cup of tea, and toast without butter is simply not the same thing! There are plenty of other examples, like raki without good company and chai without charcha. The fact that there are good pairings or things that complement each other goes well beyond food—when choosing a team, we look for complementary skills in the members of the team. Which is also why if one of them wants to leave, the other crabs may pull him/her down and not because they are jealous of this crab's good fortune. A safe borrower will look for another safe borrower as a partner if there is joint liability for loan repayment, unless, of course, they do not care about being responsible for another person's debt. In-group members might be more natural complements than out-group members: an Iyer might find his yang in another Iyer and an Iyengar in another Iyengar. Failing to recognize complementarities in the production process can have very significant consequences as Professor Michael Kremer points out in his O-ring theory of development. Similarly, winning cricket matches requires the team to have a complementary set of bowling and batting skills. And as Rosenstein-Rodan's Big Push theory argues, taking the complementarities between the different sectors of the economy into account is important for growth. Besides, since shoe thieves already know about such complementarities, failure to recognize them can have disastrous consequences for our shoes!

- ***Information matters***: Here, I do not mean to make the trivial observation that Facebook (or other social media) is important for gathering and spreading (mis-) information. Rather, it is important to realize that we operate in a world governed by information asymmetry. Firms typically must set prices without knowing what different buyers are willing to pay for their product. Moreover, one does not even need a moment's reflection to know that this information cannot be obtained by asking the buyer. The buyer will simply say that they want to pay the lowest possible price. Similarly, lenders may not know the credit worthiness of different borrowers (especially of small borrowers) and must design lending schemes in the absence of this knowledge. Depending on the setting, when hiring an employee, you may or may not know whether the other person is a shirker or a hard worker. Hence, people may engage in acts like earning a degree from an institution like AIIMS or carrying a pen in their pocket to signal their ability. Interestingly, it is also possible that you may not even be aware of your own competence in certain areas: for instance, people frequently do not know which branch of architecture is good for them. One consequence of such lack of knowledge is that you might end up joining the wrong team and pick the wrong job/technology, etc.[3] It is also important to keep in mind the platform for the delivery of information. Twitter or a telegram might require us to make our message so compact

---

[3] In that sense self-awareness is important for both the mundane and the spiritual.

that it may lose some of the essential information. On the other hand, since email does not have a word limit, there is always the danger that we might confuse the reader by providing information that is not germane to the issue at hand. Information about each other is also vital to develop the kind of opinions or beliefs we hold about others. For example, how Ram plays a Game of Chicken with Laxman may be very different from how he plays it with Ravan. And finally, the information that we gather about each other from acts like not eating that last slice of pizza determines what is common knowledge, which in turn affects how we interact with others.

- *Cognitive costs matter*: Economists typically think of rational behaviour as something that takes the marginal cost and benefits into account before making choices. This is crucially dependent on the fact that making these calculations is not costly for our brains. And yet we know that being poor affects our cognitive ability and therefore the kind of decisions we make. Similarly, while more choices may be better, if it is too costly to weigh all the options, you might be better off with fewer choices. This issue of the higher cognitive load with more choices, as we saw previously, is certainly true for the elderly. Simply put, if a restaurant's menu is too long, by the time you finish choosing your dish, it might already be time for the restaurant to close. This failure to consider the cognitive costs of decision-making can lead to a lose-lose situation. You go home hungry, and the restaurant makes no money since you did not order anything. In fact, statistical discrimination or stereotyping (without justifying it) can be thought of as mechanism that our brain uses to cut down on cognitive costs. It amounts to using a heuristic to classify people. Here is a simple rule of thumb:[4] when significant cognitive costs are involved, people often use a rule of thumb or heuristic to solve the problem. Maybe it helps to keep that in mind the next time you stereotype someone, or someone typecasts you based on your place of origin in India!

- **Strategic behaviour matters**: Whether it is the Game of Chicken or the game of cricket, it is important to reflect on how the other player may choose their actions, i.e., strategic thinking is important. The final outcome in many instances (like in a game of Tic-Tac-Toe, or a firm's pricing strategy, or an election) in our everyday lives also depends on the actions of other persons or players. Chanakya already explained this long ago in *Arthashastra*, as did Sun Tzu in *The Art of War*. Every chess player, from a novice to Grandmaster Vishwanathan Anand, will tell you that it is important to think about what your opponent will do in response to your move. Apparently, what sets players apart in chess is how far ahead they can foresee this sequence of alternating moves. Actually, whether it is gerrymandering or nuclear non-proliferation, game theory is all around us. It can even explain why religion and culture might require us to be generous with our hospitality. Since swagger (be it

---

[4] My friend and co-author Utteeyo Dasgupta has an interesting take on heuristics and rules of thumb. On one hand too few choices are bad since variety is the spice of life while too many choices make it hard to find the best options. Excess of anything, whether it is flavours of coffee or opinions, is bad. So he says think of a heuristic as the Buddha's middle path or the one that helps us get to the golden mean.

James Dean or Banno)[5] can help win games, it is important to recognize its presence and whether it is genuine or affected. This can make all the difference in a Game of Chicken. Many situations in life, like price wars or going out for dinner with friends, occur repeatedly. Trust and reputation can play an important role in such situations. Indeed, having a God of Helmets and God of the Traffic Lights might help curb some of the lawlessness we see on the roads.

To end this book where it started, all I want to say is that *economics* matters, and it matters not only in the abstract, but it matters in the little things in our personal lives and for a great many of our social interactions. In a way, economics is all around us. My hope is that, in a small way, this book has helped to clarify the importance of economic thinking and illustrate its practical relevance.

---

[5] Needless to say, Kangana Ranaut on whom this song is featured in the movie *Tanu Weds Manu Returns* has plenty of swagger.

Suggested Readings

This section aims to enhance the reader's experience by suggesting additional readings for those who wish to delve more into a topic. Sometimes, these suggestions are of a more technical nature and take a deeper dive into the material. At other times it might take you on a lateral excursion. For all cases, however, I have made every effort to provide the reader some guidance about the type of suggested reading.

To start with, let me suggest some textbooks if you wish to polish your skills in economics. These books are ordered by level of difficulty starting with the one that is the easiest to read. Note that these books are not the only ones on this topic—there are plenty of substitutes available; treat these as a guide to help you find a book.

BOOKS ON MICROECONOMICS:

Principles of Microeconomics, 8th Edition, N. Gregory Mankiw, Cengage Learning

Intermediate Microeconomics: A Modern Approach, 9th Edition, Hal R. Varian, W.W. Norton & Company

Microeconomic Theory, 1st Edition, Andreu Mas-Colell, Michael D. Whinston and Jerry R. Green, Oxford University Press

BOOKS ON GAME THEORY:

Games of Strategy, 4th Edition, Avinash K. Dixit, Susan Skeath and David H. Reiley, Jr, W.W. Norton & Company

Introduction to Game Theory, Martin J. Osborne, Oxford University Press

A Course in Game Theory, 1st Edition, Martin Osborne and Ariel Rubinstein, The MIT Press

All for One and One for All

1. Ghatak, Maitreesh and Timothy W. Guinnane (1999). 'The Economics of Lending with Joint Liability: Theory and Practice'. *Journal of Development Economics,* 60, 195–228.

    This is a survey paper, that explores the state of knowledge about joint liability lending in 1999. It is technical, easily accessible and has theoretical modelling as well as a discussion of the method in practice.

2. Yunus, Muhammad and Alan Jolis (2001). *Banker to the Poor: The Autobiography of Muhammad Yunus, Founder of the Grameen Bank*. Oxford University Press.

3. Akerlof, George (1970). 'The Market for "Lemons": Quality Uncertainty and the Market Mechanism'. *The Quarterly Journal of Economics,* 84, 488–500.

    This is the classic paper on adverse selection which shows that because of information asymmetry between buyers and sellers, the used-car market will have lower quality cars or 'lemons' instead of higher quality cars or 'peaches'. Incidentally, Akerlof did part of this work when he was visiting ISI Delhi and the institution is thanked for financial support in the paper.

4. Arrow, Kenneth (1963). 'Uncertainty and the Welfare Economics of Medical Care'. *American Economic Review*, 53, 941–73.

    One of the first papers on moral hazard.

5. Dumas, Alexandre (2007). *The Three Musketeers*. Dover Publications.

    The title of the chapter is the slogan of the musketeers.

The Economics of Video Rentals

1. Sarangi, Sudipta and Randy Verbrugge (2000). 'Late Fees and Price Discrimination'. *Economics Letters*, 69, 153–158.

   The key part of this chapter which explains how a firm can use a late fee to segment the market can be found in this paper. This paper does require some economics training to enjoy it.

2. Massoud, Nadia, Anthony Saunders and Barry Scholnick (2011). 'The Cost of Being Late? The Case of Credit Card Penalty Fees'. *Journal of Financial Stability*, 7, 49–59.

   The same idea applied to credit cards plus data to verify the model.

3. https://qz.com/144372/a-brief-illustrated-history-of-blockbuster-which-is-closing-the-last-of-its-us-stores/

   A chronological history of Blockbuster which states that in the year 2000 they made 16 per cent of their money through late fees and goes on to document how the advent of Netflix killed them.

4. https://qz.com/1062888/netflix-was-founded-20-years-ago-today-because-reed-hastings-was-late-a-returning-video/

   Interesting read on how the burden of late fees led Reed Hastings to develop Netflix.

5. Iyer, Lakshmi (2011). 'Hollywood in India: Protecting Intellectual Property (A) and (B)'. *Harvard Business School Teaching Note 711–076.*

   Harvard Business School teaching note, or case study, on Hollywood's failure to make its mark in India due to intellectual property issues.

Where Have All the Other Mangoes Gone?

1. Razzolini, Laura, William F. Shughart II and Robert D. Tollison (2003). 'On the Third Law of Demand'. *Economic Inquiry*, 41, 292–298.

Much of the material in this chapter draws on my reading of this paper by my friends Laura Razzolini and Bill Shughart.

2. Alchain, Armen A. and William R. Allen (1967). *University Economics*. Wadsworth Publishing Company.

This is a classic and a very accessible textbook. It is a pleasure to read. There is one catch though—it is not always easy to find.

In God We Trust

1. Axelrod, Robert (2006). *The Evolution of Cooperation* (Revised Edition). Basic Books.

Clarifies why repeated play can explain cooperative behaviour, reputation and trench warfare in WWI.

2. https://timesofindia.indiatimes.com/business/india-business/75-vehicle-users-in-india-dont-wear-seat-belts-leading-to-15-deaths-every-day-study/articleshow/61660232.cms

Story about a survey on seat-belt use in India published in 2018.

3. https://www.motherjones.com/politics/2011/04/denial-science-chris-mooney/

A neuroscience take on why people deny science and depend on their prayers to solve worldly problems. We try to link this behaviour with people who refuse to wear seat belts and yet offer their prayers with the hope of a safe journey.

4. Iyer, Sriya (2016). 'The New Economics of Religion'. *Journal of Economic Literature*, 54, 395–441.

This accessible reading traces the historical and sociological origins of the economics of religion, and also offers insights on religion in today's world from an economist's perspective.

How About an MP from New Jersey?

1. Bauböck, R. (2005). 'Expansive Citizenship—Voting Beyond Territory and Membership'. *PS: Political Science & Politics, 38* (4), 683–687.

   This paper studies how the challenges of migration in the modern day have undermined the traditional concepts of voting rights and citizenship in democracies. It further explains the route taken by democracies to include the votes of non-residents without affecting the traditional customs.

2. Owen, D. (2011). 'Transnational Citizenship and the Democratic State: Modes of Membership and Voting Rights'. *Critical Review of International Social and Political Philosophy, 14* (5), 641–663.

   Introduces two core topics on transnational citizenship, viz, including resident non-citizens and non-resident citizens.

3. Barasch, E. (2012). 'The Twisted History of Gerrymandering in American Politics'. *Atlantic*.

4. Iyer, L. and M. Reddy (2013). 'Redrawing the Lines: Did Political Incumbents Influence Electoral Redistricting in the World's Largest Democracy?' Harvard Business School. Working Paper 14–051.

   This paper discusses in detail the most recent attempt at gerrymandering in India.

Lessons from Stolen Shoes

1. Kremer, Michael (1993). 'The O-ring Theory of Economic Development'. *The Quarterly Journal of Economics*, 108, 551–575.

   As the title suggests, this paper shows how the weakest link can act as the bottleneck in a production process and why wages for the same work can be different in a more productive team. A more easily digestible version can be found in Kaushik Basu's *Analytical Development Economics: The Less Developed Economy Revisited* published by the MIT Press in 2003.

2. https://www.nytimes.com/2015/07/11/nyregion/the-complex-art-of-selling-and-stealing-sneakers.html

    A story on the resale of stolen sneakers from stores in Brooklyn. Ultimately, a New York version of many such weekly markets in India.

3. Rosenstein-Rodan, P.N. (1961). 'Notes on the Theory of the "Big Push"'. *Economic Development for Latin America,* 57–81. Palgrave Macmillan.

    The classic essay on why economies might need that big push to get going—an easy to read conceptual treatment of the idea.

4. Murphy, K.M., A. Shleifer and R.W. Vishny (1989). 'Industrialization and the Big Push'. *Journal of Political Economy, 97* (5), 1003–1026.

    A modern and formal treatment of Rosenstein-Rodan's idea where the inherent thought is that there may be multiple equilibria in an economy and developing only one sector will not help—it will be akin to having only the shoe for one foot. Then it uses aggregate demand spillovers to illustrate that a big push can move an economy from a bad equilibrium to a good one.

Résumés or Cereals—Packaging Matters

1. https://www.businessinsider.com/how-resumes-have-evolved-since-their-first-creation-in-1482-2011-2#web-20-5

    A piece showing the evolution of résumés using a timeline approach—there are no explanations. It claims that Leonardo De Vinci wrote the first professional resume in 1428.

2. https://www.cnbc.com/2019/07/10/an-example-of-the-perfect-resume-according-to-harvard-career-experts.html

Job seekers pay attention: An example of a perfect resume by Harvard career experts.

3. https://www.hindustantimes.com/music/bollywood-puts-hit-songs-in-new-bottles-re-make-of-it-what-you-will/story-oRBBIqwIQj1kbAL8tpzQqI.html

    A rather interesting account of Bollywood's remaking of old songs—its challenges and why do they do it. In some ways, it is old wine in new bottles and not really piracy since most remakes are done legally. Of course, if only the tune is copied without attribution and not the lyrics, it becomes a legal Gordian knot.

4. Hotelling, H. (1929). 'Stability in Competition'. *Economic Journal*, 39, 41–57.

    The classic paper that started the analysis of product differentiation.

5. Economides, Nicholas (1986). 'Minimal and Maximal Product Differentiation in Hotelling's Duopoly'. *Economics Letters* 21.1, 67–71.

    This short paper generalizes Hotelling's model to a large class of utility functions.

6. Scherer, François M. (1979). 'The Welfare Economics of Product Variety: An Application to the Ready-to-eat Cereals Industry'. *The Journal of Industrial Economics*, 113–134.

    A paper on breakfast cereals that evaluates whether the endless proliferation of variety is a good or a bad thing for consumers and producers.

A Tale of Two Bounties

1. Vann, Michael G. (2003). 'Of Rats, Rice, and Race: The Great Hanoi Rat Massacre, an Episode in French Colonial History'. *French Colonial History*, 4 (1), 191–203.

This is an account of the rodent story, and makes a fascinating read.

2. Miniter, Richard (1999). 'The False Promise of Slave Redemption'. *Atlantic Monthly*, 284.1, 63–70.

    The tale of how the efforts of CSI went in vain in Sudan.

3. De Mesquita, E.B. (2005). 'The Terrorist Endgame: A Model with Moral Hazard and Learning'. *Journal of Conflict Resolution*, 49 (2), 237–258.

    A game of learning in which a government tries to negotiate with a terrorist organization.

4. https://www.mikeshor.com/courses/gametheory/docs/topic6/strangelove.html

    A website maintained by co-author Dr Mike Shor at University of Connecticut with the game theory behind the entire Dr Strangelove bit—with the transcript. Of course, you could simply watch the movie!

5. https://www.news18.com/news/opinion/as-jet-airways-crisis-exposes-moral-hazard-of-state-run-banks-privatisation-is-the-answer-2111539.html

    There are many such events—just type bailouts into a search engine. This one about the Jet Airways crisis and the State Bank of India is simply closer home.

6. https://www.gutenberg.org/files/18343/18343-h/18343-h.htm

    There are many versions of Robert Browning's poem 'The Pied Piper of Hamelin', but this is my favorite because of the illustrations. The icing on the cake is that it is free.

7. Schwarcz, Steven L. (2017). 'Too Big to Fool: Moral Hazard, Bailouts, and Corporate Responsibility'. *Minnesota Law Review*, 102, 761–802.

Although the classic paper on this topic by Kenneth Arrow was published in the *American Economic Review* in 1963, this is a good read on the too-big-to-fail perspective covered in the chapter.

Why We Should Pay Our Domestic Help More

1. Katz, L.F. (1986). 'Efficiency Wage Theories: A Partial Evaluation'. *NBER Macroeconomics Annual*, 1, 235–276.

    A bit dated but an excellent survey of efficiency wage models.

2. Raff, D.M. and L.H. Summers (1987). 'Did Henry Ford Pay Efficiency Wages?' *Journal of Labor Economics*, 5 (4, Part 2), S57–S86.

    The proof of the pudding, they say, is in the eating—this paper does the job for the Henry Ford hypothesis using actual data.

3. Goldsmith, Arthur H., Jonathan R. Veum and William Darity Jr (2000). 'Working Hard for the Money? Efficiency Wages and Worker Effort'. *Journal of Economic Psychology*, 21.4, 351–385.

    This is the test of the efficiency wage hypothesis under controlled conditions in a lab.

4. Menon, Nidhiya and Yana Van Der Meulen Rodgers (2017). 'The Impact of the Minimum Wage on Male and Female Employment and Earnings in India'. *Asian Development Review*, 34.1, 28–64.

    Parsing the minimum wage question from the gender perspective using Indian data. It finds that minimum wage rates increase earnings in the rural sector, especially for men, without any employment losses. Minimum wage rates also increase the residual gender wage gap, which may be explained by weaker compliance among firms that hire female workers.

Where the Mind Does Not Work

1. https://www.vox.com/2016/6/6/11852640/cartoon-poor-neighborhoods

    Sketches the history of racial divide and how that led to a dual society of black and white neighbourhoods in the US—giving way to poverty and various social and mental ailments in various forms.

2. Miller, G.A. (1956). 'The Magical Number Seven, Plus or Minus Two: Some Limits on Our Capacity for Processing Information'. *Psychological Review*, *63* (2), 81.

3. Deck, Cary and Sudipta Sarangi (2009). 'Inducing Imperfect Recall in the Lab'. *Journal of Economic Behavior & Organization*, 69.1, 64–74.

    We conduct an experiment in this paper to induce imperfect recall—ensure that people cannot recall what they did just a while ago without using intoxicants, but rely on divided attention.

4. Mani, A., S. Mullainathan, E. Shafir and J. Zhao (2013). 'Poverty Impedes Cognitive Function'. *Science*, *341* (6149), 976–980.

    This is the study on which the chapter is based.

5. https://www.princeton.edu/news/2013/08/29/poor-concentration-poverty-reduces-brainpower-needed-navigating-other-areas-life

    The quotes from the authors in the essay are from this news article.

Pens in Pockets

1. Spence, M. (1981). 'Signaling, Screening, and Information'. *Studies in Labor Markets*. University of Chicago Press. 319–358.

    Introduces signalling in an easy-to-follow manner. In order to distinguish themselves, job seekers can invest in education to signal their quality or ability as well as variations of this theme. Spence is also credited with the idea of screening which is covered here as well. If, however, you like classic papers, then the following paper is easy to read as well.

2. Michael, Spence (1973). 'Job Market Signaling'. *Quarterly Journal of Economics*, 87.3, 355–374.

3. peneconomics.com/blog/2015/7/3/status-symbols

Fascinating read on how pens are used as a status symbol. This also explains pens as a Veblen good.

4. Debroy, Bibek (2020), *A Fountain Pen Story*. Observer Research Foundation. https://www.orfonline.org/wp-content/uploads/2020/06/ORF-Monograph-Fountain-Pen-Story.pdf

The quote comparing Gandhi and Ambedkar's attitudes to fountain pens comes from this fascinating read about fountain pens by Bibek Debroy, who himself is an ardent collector of this writing instrument.

5. Bhagat, Chetan (2004). *Five Point Someone: What Not to Do at IIT*. Rupa Publications Private Limited.

Food for thought vis-à-vis signalling. A story about when signalling can be noisy, because you go to an IIT but come out at the bottom of the class.

Telegram. An Obituary. Stop

1. https://thediplomat.com/2013/06/india-sends-its-last-telegram-stop/

Accounts for the legacy of the telegram in India with relevant statistics and finally its demise on 15 July 2013 after 163 years of service.

2. 'Symantec Corporation'. *Internet Security Threat Report* 2014. Volume 18.

3. Shapiro, Carl and Hal R. Varian (1998). *Information Rules: A Strategic Guide to the Network Economy*. Harvard Business Press.

An excellent and easy to read book about the differences between fixed cost and variable cost, and how they effect the production and pricing of information goods, i.e., products that are valuable because of their content.

4. Gal, Michal S. and Daniel L. Rubinfeld (2016). 'The Hidden Costs of Free Goods: Implications for Antitrust Enforcement'. *Antitrust Law Journal*, 80.3, 521–562.

A paper that illustrates that free goods may not always be good for society.

5. Rao, Justin M. and David H. Reiley (2012). 'The Economics of Spam'. *Journal of Economic Perspectives*, 26.3, 87–110

Rereading an Old Gandhi Essay

1. http://www.bbc.com/travel/story/20190325-the-birthplace-of-gandhis-peaceful-protest

This is an excellent piece on the Pietermaritzburg incident and what happened next—perfect background reading.

2. Poinsot, P. (2016). 'Jules Dupuit and the Railroads: What is the Role of the State?'. *Journal of the History of Economic Thought, 38* (2), 189–209.

A very perceptive and easy read of Dupuit's thoughts on railroad travel.

3. Tirole, Jean (1988). *The Theory of Industrial Organization*. MIT Press.

The Dupuit quote in the chapter can be found in this textbook on price discrimination and other topics relating to industrial organization. For those who want to test their French the original paper is 'De l'influence des peages sur l'utilite des voies de communication', (1849), *Annales des ponts et chaussées,* Vol.17 (1 sem), 170–248.

4. Rosen, S. and A.M. Rosenfield (1997). 'Ticket Pricing'. *The Journal of Law and Economics, 40* (2), 351–376.

A formal treatment of ticket pricing for different classes of travel under different assumptions. To start with, the paper assumes that total or aggregate demand is known, but individual preferences of travellers is not known to the firm.

The Many Shades of Prejudice: A Look at the US and India

1. Arrow, K.J. (1998). 'What Has Economics to Say about Racial Discrimination?'. *Journal of Economic Perspectives*, *12* (2), 91–100.

This focuses on understanding prejudices borne out of preconceived notions towards people from other castes, religion, colour and even places of residences. It is in the nature of an accessible survey.

2. Mesic, A., L. Franklin, A. Cansever, F. Potter, A. Sharma, A. Knopov and M. Siegel (2018). 'The Relationship between Structural Racism and Black-White Disparities in Fatal Police Shootings at the State Level'. *Journal of the National Medical Association*, *110* (2), 106–116.

About race and law enforcement using state-level data from the US. The paper finds that structural racism is an important predictor of the black–white disparity in rates of police shootings of unarmed victims across states.

3. Becker, Gary S. (2010). *The Economics of Discrimination*. University of Chicago Press.

Becker's work (and more) on discrimination summarized by Becker himself. Insightful read.

4. Bertrand, Marianne and Sendhil Mullainathan (2004). 'Are Emily and Greg More Employable than Lakisha and Jamal?: A Field Experiment on Labor Market Discrimination'. *American Economic Review*, 94.4, 991–1013.

What's in a name—apparently a lot!

5. Banerjee, A., M. Bertrand, S. Datta and S. Mullainathan (2009). 'Labor Market Discrimination in Delhi: Evidence from a Field Experiment'. *Journal of Comparative Economics*, *37* (1), 14–27.

    The same question studied in the previous paper, but in the Indian context where diversity is much greater. So in some ways, this makes for a more interesting read.

6. https://www.theguardian.com/education/2011/jan/11/learning-english-india-dalits-rahman

    Interesting article on the Dalit community's devotion and their expectation out of the English language. It talks about the Goddess of English as the one who will liberate them from poverty, ignorance and oppression. So perhaps my hypothesizing for a God of Seat Belts is not entirely fanciful.

Capturing Indian 'Crab' Behaviour

1. Menon, Tanya and Leigh Thompson (2010). 'Envy at Work'. *Harvard Business Review*, 88.4, 74–79.
2. Duffy, Michelle K. and Jason D. Shaw (2000). 'The Salieri Syndrome: Consequences of Envy in Groups'. *Small Group Research*, 31.1, 3–23.

    These two papers examine different aspects of envy—one in the workplace while the other one in groups, and how it affects performance.

3. Chen, Yan and Sherry Xin Li (2009). 'Group Identity and Social Preferences'. *American Economic Review*, 99.1, 431–57.

    The in-group and out-group business examined using controlled lab experiments.

4. Ratliff, Kate A. and Shigehiro Oishi (2013). 'Gender Differences in Implicit Self-Esteem Following a Romantic Partner's Success or Failure'. *Journal of Personality and Social Psychology*, 105.4, 688.

    Bringing it closer home: self-esteem of males and females in a relationship. The key finding is that men felt worse about themselves and the future of their relationships when their female partner did better. Why should you read it? The last line in the abstract says it all: 'These gender differences have important implications for understanding social comparison in romantic relationships.'

Earthquake Economics

1. Anbarci, N., M. Escaleras and C.A. Register (2005). 'Earthquake Fatalities: The Interaction of Nature and Political Economy'. *Journal of Public Economics*, *89* (9–10), 1907–1933.
2. Escaleras, M., N. Anbarci and C.A. Register (2007). 'Public Sector Corruption and Major Earthquakes: A Potentially Deadly Interaction'. *Public Choice*, *132* (1–2), 209–230.

Nejat Anbarci's papers on earthquakes are cited in the essay.

3. https://www.brookings.edu/blog/future-development/2018/02/07/development-self-interest-and-the-countries-left-behind/

A brief account of how foreign aid usually works.

4. Escaleras, M. and C. Register (2016). 'Public Sector Corruption and Natural Hazards'. *Public Finance Review*, *44* (6), 746–768.

More on the claim that corruption exacerbates the destruction from a natural catastrophe into a disaster where death tolls are even higher.

5. https://www.econlib.org/library/Enc/CreativeDestruction.html

A relatively short and fascinating read on Joseph Schumpeter's theory of 'creative destruction'. If you wish to pursue the original you need to go to his book, *Capitalism, Socialism, and Democracy* (1942).

Palaces, Raki and Game Theory

1. Jackson, Matthew O. (2019). *The Human Network: How Your Social Position Determines Your Power, Beliefs, and Behaviors*. Vintage.

A fascinating introduction to networks.

2. http://competitionandappropriation.com/wp-content/ uploads/2017/08/HistoryGameTheory.pdf

   Paul Walker has written many timeline versions of the history of game theory. This is a more up-to-date one. For information about the Nobel Prize winners mentioned in the essay, you can look up the Nobel Foundation press releases.

3. https://www.cnn.com/travel/article/turkey-signature-drink-raki/ index.html

   CNN has provided a guide to drinking Raki. To learn more about Turkey, feel free to use standard guidebooks like Lonely Planet, DK's Rough Guides or Frommer's travel guides.

Facebook against Corruption

1. Schelling, Thomas C. (1980). *The Strategy of Conflict.* Harvard University Press, 1980.

   To quote Roger Myerson from a paper published in the *Journal of Economic Literature* in 2009, 'Thomas Schelling's *The Strategy of Conflict* is a masterpiece that should be recognized as one of the most important and influential books in social theory.'

2. Jha, C.K. and S. Sarangi (2017). 'Does Social Media Reduce Corruption?' *Information Economics and Policy*, 39, 60–71.

   The material in this chapter on social media and lower corruption is drawn from this paper. An accessible version of this paper can be found at: http://eprints.lse.ac.uk/81976/1/ Can%20social%20media%20and%20the%20internet%20 reduce%20corruption_%20-%20IGC.pdf

3. Howard, P.N., A. Duffy, D. Freelon, M.M. Hussain, W. Mari and M. Maziad (2011). 'Opening Closed Regimes: What Was the Role of Social Media During the Arab Spring?' Available at SSRN: https://ssrn.com/abstract=2595096 or http://dx.doi. org/10.2139/ssrn.2595096

4. https://voxeu.org/article/riots-and-revolutions-digital-age

Basically, the title of this piece, 'Riots, Revolutions, Democratisation, and Information Cascades' says it all. It is a very interesting read on popular movements and how they snowball.

Chicken: The Game Politicians Love to Play

1. Rapoport, A and A.M. Chammah (1966). 'The Game of Chicken'. *American Behavioral Scientist*, 10.3, 10–28.

A very nice introduction to the Game of Chicken.

2. Russell, B. (1959). *Common Sense and Nuclear Warfare*. Routledge.

The source of the Russell quote. Generally, I do not refer to Wikipedia in my suggested readings since I assume that the reader can find this on their own. However, for this chapter I will make an exception and state that the entry for the Game of Chicken is quite instructive.

The First Piece of Cake . . .

1. Andreoni, J. (1990). 'Impure Altruism and Donations to Public Goods: A Theory of Warm-Glow Giving'. *Economic Journal*, 100.401, 464-477.

The classic paper on warm glow and why people give to public goods.

2. https://medicalxpress.com/news/2018-09-kindness-real.html

Research at University of Sussex proposing that warm glow from generous decisions is real by studying brain activity.

3. Mauss, M. (2000). *The Gift: The Form and Reason for Exchange in Archaic Societies*. W. W. Norton & Company.

A fascinating book about the reasons behind gift giving—it is also the seminal work on this topic.

4. Brams, S.J. and A.D. Taylor (1996). *Fair Division: From Cake-Cutting to Dispute Resolution*. Cambridge University Press.

It is amazing how many papers have been written about sharing a cake in a fair way. This book provides an introduction to this and other related issues.

The Last Piece of Cake . . .

1. https://www.startribune.com/why-won-t-anyone-in-minnesota-take-the-last-piece-of-food/510139261/
2. https://presbyterianblues.wordpress.com/2013/05/25/the-international-phenomenon-of-the-last-piece/

These two readings are stories about the last piece in Minnesota and around the world.

3. https://www.cbsnews.com/news/police-man-fatally-stabbed-over-last-piece-of-chicken/

The crazy story of the fight over the last piece of chicken!

4. https://plato.stanford.edu/entries/common-knowledge/

The link to the Stanford Encyclopedia of Philosophy entry on Common Knowledge.

5. Chwe, Michael Suk-Young (2013). *Rational Ritual: Culture, Coordination, and Common Knowledge*. Princeton University Press.

This is on rituals and common knowledge—a book that has economics, anthropology, movies—something for all tastes.

6. Aumann, R.J. (1976). 'Agreeing to Disagree'. *The Annals of Statistics*, 1236–1239.
7. Lewis, D. (2008). *Convention: A Philosophical Study*. John Wiley & Sons.

The first reading is a formal model of common knowledge and the second reading provides a philosophical understanding of common knowledge.

8. Schelling, T.C. (1958). 'The Strategy of Conflict. Prospectus for a Reorientation of Game Theory'. *Journal of Conflict Resolution*, *2* (3), 203–264.

   Everything you wanted to know about focal points.

9. Basu, Kaushik (2018). *The Republic of Beliefs: A New Approach to Law and Economics*. Princeton University Press.

   On how beliefs matter for economic behaviour, especially strategic behaviour and in the context of law and economics.

For a Few Overs More

1. Cannonier, C., B. Panda and S. Sarangi (2015). '20-Over versus 50-Over Cricket: Is There a Difference?' *Journal of Sports Economics*, *16* (7), 760–783.

   The research on which this essay is based.

2. https://www.livemint.com/Sundayapp/ vWgCJuzycYOyzzAckWoycI/Want-to-stop-tampering-Use-our-balls-says-UK-manufacturer.html

   On the difference between cricket ball brands and their propensity for tampering.

Are More Choices Really Better?

1. Besedeš, Tibor, Cary Deck, Sudipta Sarangi and Mikhael Shor (2012). 'Age Effects and Heuristics in Decision Making'. *Review of Economics and Statistics*, 94, No. 2, 580–595.

   The research on which this essay is based.

2. Schwartz, Barry (2004). *The Paradox of Choice: Why More is Less*. Harper Perennial.

   Very much in line with the topic, but from the point of view of psychology—not a study on incentivized decisions. The basic idea is that even too many choices can leave people feeling anxious and depressed, both during and after decision making.

3. Iyengar, Sheena (2010). *The Art of Choosing*. Little, Brown.

    A fascinating book about the how and why of choice.

4. https://www.nytimes.com/2010/02/27/your-money/27shortcuts.html

    If you want to skip the books but still get a whiff of the research . . .

P.G. Wodehouse, Futurist

1. http://www.gutenberg.org/files/8178/8178-h/8178-h.htm#link2H_4_0004

    Link to the short story 'International Affair' in *The Politeness of Princess and Other Stories*.

2. Wodehouse Society UK: https://www.pgwodehousesociety.org.uk/

    Official Wodehouse page.

3. https://www.theguardian.com/books/2002/jul/20/classics.pgwodehouse

    On India's love affair with Wodehouse—an essay by Sashi Tharoor.

In Freedom Begins Responsibilities

1. Defoe, Daniel (2003). *A Journal of the Plague Year*. Penguin Classics.

    A somewhat depressing read in the times of Covid-19, but reveals how investigative journalism came about.

2. Fair, Ray C. (1978). 'The Effect of Economic Events on Votes for President'. *Review of Economics and Statistics*, 60(2), 159–173.

The relationship between economic activity and election outcomes—applied to the United States. The rationale should work for other countries as well.

3.   Brender, A. and A. Drazen (2008). 'How Do Budget Deficits and Economic Growth Affect Reelection Prospects? Evidence from a Large Panel of Countries'. *American Economic Review*, 98 (5), 2203–2220.

More on economics and election—but using data from a large number of countries.

4.   Sen, Amartya (1977). 'Starvation and Exchange Entitlements: A General Approach and Its Application to the Great Bengal Famine'. *Cambridge Journal of Economics* 1.1, 33–59.

A paper that shapes our understanding of famines in modern times—essentially, that they are man-made.

5.   Luo, Shaowen, Kwok Ping Tsang and Zichao Yang (2020). 'The Impact of Stay-at-Home Orders on US Output: A Network Perspective'. Available at SSRN: https://ssrn.com/abstract=3571866 or http://dx.doi.org/10.2139/ssrn.3571866

This paper provides the dollar value of the lockdown in the US for a specific time period using an approach that takes the interdependencies in production into account.